THE
COOK-AHEAD
COOKBOOK

Cynthia MacGregor

BRISTOL PUBLISHING ENTERPRISES

San Leandro, California

A nitty gritty® Cookbook

Printed in the United States of America.

ISBN: 1-55867-270-2

Cover design: Frank J. Paredes
Cover photography: John A. Benson
Food stylist: Susan Devaty
Illustrator: Hannah Suhr

CONTENTS

DEDICATION
For Justin, Tori, Steffan and Aiden

ACKNOWLEDGMENTS

Thanks to my mother, Yvonne Epstein, who instilled in me my love of cooking and good food and who contributed recipes to this book.

Thanks to Jesse Leaf for practical information, a few recipes and advice and encouragement.

Thanks to all the others who shared a recipe or several with me.

Last but not least, a heartfelt thank you to the staff of the Publix supermarket at Meadows Square in Lantana, and especially Rocky, Dave and their staff in the meat department — and to Joy as well.

COMMON PROBLEMS — AND A PLAN

An unexpected change in your schedule, unexpected guests, or simply low energy are all good reasons to have a fall-back entrée in your freezer. If you avoid takeout, for reasons of economy or taste, and you don't care for commercially prepared frozen entrées, this book offers a relatively easy, home-cooked solution.

The following pages are about cooking main courses and storing them for future meals. It's the main course that normally requires the most thought, time and preparation, and it's the main course upon which most people will judge your dinner, whether we're talking about guests, your family or yourself.

In this book, you'll find recipes for main dishes featuring poultry (chicken or turkey), beef, veal, pork, sausages and lamb. There are more recipes for poultry because it's healthy, it's budget-minded and there are so many things you can do with it.

Not every dinner can be prepared ahead and frozen with the same degree of success, and you won't find recipes for them here. Steaks and roasts are not great candidates for freezing. Neither are foods containing sour cream, yogurt or mayonnaise. Breaded coatings are often soggy when reheated.

All the dishes in this cookbook freeze nicely in single-serving packages and can be microwaved or reheated on top of the stove or in the oven with great results.

SIDE DISHES AND VEGETABLES

If your entrée is already prepared, the side dish is easy. A baked potato goes with many meat dishes, and there's nothing easier to fix. Rice is simple and quick, and you can dress up rice quickly and easily by cooking it in chicken broth instead of water and sprinkling in a little thyme and sage, or thyme and rosemary, or fresh-cut dill. Or make a simple pasta, or bulgur, barley, beans or corn.

The vegetable dish is equally easy to deal with. My favorite answer is to whip up a quick salad—lettuce and other raw vegetables, oil and vinegar, herbs and garlic, salt and pepper. You may prefer a more complex creation. Or serve a fresh steamed vegetable. Even if you prefer fresh vegetables to frozen, keeping a few boxes or bags of frozen vegetables on hand is a good idea.

In some cases, such as in some of the stews, the vegetables and starch are already in the meal, and you don't have to prepare anything else at all, though you may want to offer a salad or some garlic bread for a bit of variety.

HERBS

Generally speaking you can substitute fresh herbs, if you have them on hand, for dried herbs called for in these recipes; just triple the amounts. But *do not* substitute dried dill where fresh dill is called for.

CONTAINERS

There are many commercially produced containers available in which you can successfully freeze your dinners. If you plan to microwave your dinners in the containers, they must be microwavable. Keep several sizes of containers on hand. Plastic freezer bags are good for some dishes. Because I usually transfer the entrée to a saucepan to reheat on the stovetop, I find used margarine tubs to be convenient containers.

Do not fill your container completely full, as foods, especially sauces and other liquids, expand when they freeze. Do fill the container almost full—excess air is your enemy—but leave a bit of room for expansion.

For food safety reasons, freeze your creations quickly rather than cooling them on the counter or stove. However, do not take a container full of food freshly hot from the oven or stove and place it so that it is resting on another container in the freezer, or has another container resting on it. If you can't place it on an empty space on the freezer shelf, your next best option is to cool it in the refrigerator and then place it in the freezer.

In the instructions I have included with each recipe, I usually recommend one freezing method for that recipe: "freeze in containers," or "freeze in plastic freezer bags," or "freeze tightly wrapped in aluminum foil." With most of the recipes earmarked for aluminum foil freezing, you really ought to adhere to the suggestion; but in many cases, the question of plastic bags vs. containers is a toss-up.

There are labels available that are intended specifically for use on frozen food packages. Label packages with the contents and the date that you froze them.

STORAGE TIME LIMITS

The United States Department of Agriculture recommends keeping cooked meat dishes for a maximum of two to three months and cooked chicken for four to six months (six if it's covered in gravy or sauce). Beyond those times, the flavors and textures will begin to degrade. I have exceeded those limits often, especially when a dish is frozen in a sauce, with good results. There are many variables that affect whether a dish will keep well beyond the recommended time: How many times a day or a week is your freezer door opened? How much air is in the container? Does the dish have a sauce? How well packed is your freezer?

Here are some guidelines:

- Freezers, unlike refrigerators, function best when they're tightly packed.
- Excess air in your storage container will hasten the deterioration of your foods. If storing in a freezer bag, squeeze the air out of the bag before you seal it.
- If a dish has little or no sauce in it, consider keeping it less than the recommended time.

REHEATING FROZEN FOODS

It is not necessary to thaw foods before reheating, though you may safely do so (in the refrigerator, not at room temperature) if you wish. If you do thaw foods, decrease the reheating time accordingly. Times given in this book are for defrosting *frozen* packages of food.

Every recipe will give suggestions for reheating, but here are some guidelines:

- 325°–350° is a good oven heat for reheating
- a covered pot on a medium-low burner is a good rule for stovetop reheating
- 70% power is a good setting for microwave reheating

I usually prefer to heat on the stove, rather than the other two options. Obviously, it will take longer to heat enough servings of any recipe to feed four or six people than it will to heat just one for yourself. Also, "medium-low" (or any other setting) on your stove may not produce identical heat to medium-low on another person's stove. And your cookware makes a difference too—not all saucepans, skillets or Dutch ovens heat at the same rate or evenness. Where I've called for reheating in a covered pot, use a medium saucepan for smaller quantities and a Dutch oven or similar larger pot if you're reheating four or six portions. Do this especially if it's a dish that contains not only meat but vegetables and potatoes too, or a large quantity of sauce.

To reheat on the stovetop, remove food from the container and place in a pot with about ¼ cup water or another liquid in the recipe, such as wine or broth. Cover and cook over medium-low heat for about 25 to 30 minutes or until heated through. Stir and check once or twice during reheating process, adding more water if the liquid level gets too low. If reheating three or more servings, 5 or 10 additional minutes' reheating time may be needed.

To reheat in the microwave, use 50% or 70% microwave power — 70% is usually a good choice — and heat for 2 minutes. At the end of 2 minutes, check to see how well-heated the food is, and stir so that ingredients are moved from the center of the dish to the edges, if possible. Microwave for another minute or so, depending on the food, number of portions you are reheating and your oven's power. You can restart the microwave as many times as you need to. It is better to err on the side of caution than risk ruining your dinner. Meat and poultry will toughen if overcooked. Stir the food each time you check it. If your container is microwave-safe, you can reheat the food in it. Otherwise, transfer food to a microwave-safe dish.

HOW TO FILL YOUR FREEZER WITH HOME COOKING

First plan: Prepare any recipe in this book for your evening's dinner, to serve immediately. But cook double what you need. Freeze half the batch to have on hand for that inevitable situation when you'll need to grab something out of the freezer. Do that often enough, with enough different recipes, and the contents of your freezer will soon be the envy of all your friends and neighbors.

Second plan: Set aside a cooking day, or half a day, every so often. Make three recipes; make six; make more. The only boundaries are how much time you have to be in the kitchen, how much food your freezer will hold, and how quickly you think you can use it.

SHORTCUTS

There are only a few recipes in this book that involve a can of soup as an ingredient, but there are other shortcuts that I believe in and take full advantage of, even when they cost a little more. If you spend time, you save money, but if you spend money, you can save time.

One of these shortcuts is sliced mushrooms — I seldom buy whole ones for a recipe that calls for sliced mushrooms. If my supermarket has fresh sliced mushrooms, I'll pay the premium to save slicing time. If you'd rather save the money, an egg slicer will slice mushrooms quite nicely, and a good deal faster than a knife. For convenience, chopped garlic can be found in bottles in your supermarket, but I do not recommend it, as the flavor is not the same. Black olives can be purchased already sliced. Packaged diced ham is sold in most supermarkets. Keep your eye open for other time-saving prepared ingredients.

Another time-saver is meat that's cut to order. If you shop at a customer-friendly supermarket, your butcher can be your best ally. In my supermarket, there is no extra charge for cutting meat to the shopper's specifications. If I need chicken cut into 2-inch squares, or cubed beef, or veal chops that are extra-thick, I only need to ask.

Now you have a battle plan. Choose from the following recipes and get ready to do some cooking. You'll never be caught short again. And you'll love the tastiness (and ease!) of the solution.

CHICKEN AND TURKEY

EASY SWEET 'N' HOT CHICKEN

This chicken dish is so easy you may wind up feeling guilty — with this recipe, almost no work results in a delicious main course. This goes nicely with rice.

1 1/2 cups commercially prepared picante sauce (hot salsa sauce)
1 tbs. Dijon mustard
1 tsp. ground ginger
1/4 tsp. dried savory
1 tsp. lemon juice
4 boneless, skinless chicken breast halves

Heat oven to 350°. Put all ingredients except chicken in a baking dish big enough to hold all 4 pieces of chicken in one layer. Mix well. Add chicken.

Bake for 30 to 40 minutes or until largest piece of chicken is done when tested with a knife.

Freeze in containers or plastic freezer bags.

To reheat on the stovetop or in the microwave, see pages 5 and 6.

SULTAN'S DELIGHT ARABIAN CHICKEN

Servings: 4

Legend has it that an ancient Arabian sultan fed this dish to all the new wives in his harem, and they were many. He restricted them to one serving so they wouldn't go to sleep after dinner!

1 tbs. canola oil or other oil
2 small onions, cut into medium-thick slices
4 boneless, skinless chicken breast halves
2 cups chicken broth
1 cup dry white wine
1/4 cup brown sugar, packed
1 small lime, thinly sliced
1 tbs. curry powder
1/2 cup smooth peanut butter, prefer no additives
1 apple, cored, seeded and cut into eighths, prefer Granny Smith or other tart variety
1/3 cup slivered almonds
1 cup dates

In a nonstick pan, heat oil over medium heat. Add onion slices. Stir to separate and turn, cooking until translucent. Add chicken, cooking until lightly browned on both sides. Add broth, wine, brown sugar, lime and curry powder, and simmer for 10 minutes.

Remove chicken from pan and set aside. Add peanut butter to pan. Stir until blended, add apples and cook for 1 minute. Return chicken to pan, cook for 3 minutes and remove from heat. Add almonds and dates.

Freeze in containers or plastic freezer bags.

To reheat on the stovetop or in the microwave, see pages 5 and 6.

LIME CHICKEN

Servings: 4

Here's a nice variation of the traditional lemon chicken—instead of lemons, this recipe uses limes for a slightly different flavor.

1 chicken, quartered, or 4 favorite pieces (breast or leg quarters)
salt, freshly ground pepper and paprika to taste
2 tbs. vegetable oil
1 cup chicken broth
2 tbs. soy sauce
3 cloves garlic, sliced
4 green onions, green and white parts, sliced
1/4 cup grated fresh ginger
1/2 tsp. dried thyme
1/2 tsp. dried sage
1 red bell pepper, sliced
4 slices fresh lime
1/3 cup slivered almonds

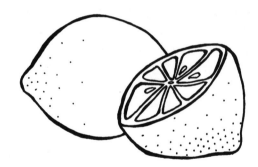

Heat oven to 350°. Season chicken with salt, pepper and paprika. In a large skillet, heat oil over medium heat. Place chicken in skillet skin-side down and cook until skin is nicely brown.

While chicken is browning, pour broth into a baking pan large enough to hold chicken pieces. Add soy sauce, garlic, green onions, ginger, thyme, sage and red pepper. Stir.

When chicken is browned, transfer to baking pan, skin-side up. Tuck a slice of lime under skin of each piece. Bake for 45 to 50 minutes, or until chicken tests done. Add almonds before serving.

Freeze in plastic freezer bags.

To reheat on the stovetop or in the microwave, see pages 5 and 6.

SUNRISE CHICKEN WITH GINGER AND ORANGE

Servings: 4

Don't be daunted by the number of ingredients; the prep is really easy and the flavor is a winner.

4 boneless, skinless chicken breast
   halves
salt and freshly ground pepper to taste
1 tbs. canola oil
2 tsp. grated fresh ginger
1 cup orange juice
1/2 cup dry white wine
1 tsp. lime juice

1/2 tsp. Dijon mustard
1 tsp. maple syrup
1/2 tsp. dried thyme
1/4 tsp. dried coriander
1 can (15 oz.) sweet potatoes, drained
1/3 cup slivered almonds
1 cup dates

Season chicken with salt and pepper. Heat oil in a large skillet over medium heat. Add chicken, cooking until lightly browned on both sides. Add ginger, orange juice, wine, lime juice, mustard, maple syrup, thyme and coriander. Stir to blend. Add sweet potatoes. Simmer for 10 minutes. Remove from heat and add almonds and dates.

Freeze in plastic freezer bags or large containers.

To reheat on the stovetop or in the microwave, see pages 5 and 6.

BASQUE CHICKEN

The Basque region straddles the Pyrenees mountain range, bordering south-western France and northern Spain. It has a distinctive, hearty cuisine with elements of both French and Spanish cooking.

1 chicken, quartered, or 4 favorite
   pieces (leg or breast quarters)
2 cloves garlic, minced
salt and freshly ground pepper to taste
3 tbs. olive oil
1/2 lb. mushrooms, sliced
1 medium tomato, diced

1 red bell pepper, diced
1 green bell pepper, diced
2 medium onions, diced
2 tbs. capers with 1 tsp. caper brine
1 1/2 cups stuffed green olives
1 cup pitted black olives
2 bay leaves

Rub chicken with garlic, salt and pepper. Refrigerate, covered, for 1 hour.

Heat oil in a large skillet over medium heat. Brown chicken well on both sides. Remove chicken from pan and set aside. Add mushrooms to pan, sautéing until lightly browned. Return chicken to pan and add all remaining ingredients. Reduce heat, cover pan and simmer for 30 to 40 minutes, or until chicken tests done. Remove bay leaves.

Freeze in plastic freezer bags.

To reheat on the stovetop or in the microwave, see pages 5 and 6.

LEMON CHICKEN FLORENTINE

The spinach and fresh ginger in this recipe make it a little different from the typical lemon chicken recipe.

1 chicken, quartered, or 4 favorite pieces (leg or breast quarters)
salt and freshly ground pepper to taste
2 tbs. olive oil or other oil
2 cups chicken broth
1/2 cup dry white wine
2 tbs. grated fresh ginger
2 onions, sliced
4 cloves garlic, sliced
1 tsp. dried thyme
1 tsp. dried sage
1 tsp. dried rosemary
4 slices lemon
about 1/2 lb. fresh spinach, washed and drained

Heat oven to 350°. Season chicken with salt and pepper to taste. Heat oil over medium heat in a large skillet. Add chicken to skillet skin-side down and cook until browned.

Pour broth into a large baking pan and add wine, ginger, onions, garlic, thyme, sage and rosemary. Mix well.

As chicken pieces become browned, place them skin-side up in baking pan. Tuck 1 lemon slice under skin of each chicken piece. When all chicken pieces are browned, place baking pan in oven and cook for 35 minutes or until chicken tests done.

Remove pan from oven and tuck spinach around chicken. Return to oven for another 2 minutes.

Freeze in plastic freezer bags.

To reheat on the stovetop or in the microwave, see pages 5 and 6.

CHICKEN BREASTS
WITH TOMATOES AND CAPERS

Capers lend a distinctive flavor to many dishes.

4 boneless, skinless chicken breast halves
salt and freshly ground pepper to taste
1 tbs. olive oil
1 tbs. butter
2 shallots, finely chopped
2 cloves garlic, finely chopped
3 green onions, white and green parts, sliced

1 can (14.5 oz.) diced tomatoes, with juice
2 tbs. red wine vinegar
$1/2$ cup dry white wine
2 tsp. tomato paste
$1/4$ cup capers with 1 tsp. caper brine
1 tsp. dried tarragon
$1/8$ cup chopped fresh dill

Season chicken with salt and pepper. Heat oil and butter over medium heat in a large skillet. Sauté chicken on both sides until lightly browned. Add shallots, garlic and green onions and cook just until wilted.

Add remaining ingredients, blending thoroughly. Bring to a boil, reduce heat and simmer for 15 minutes, or until chicken tests done.

Freeze in containers.

To reheat on the stovetop or in the microwave, see pages 5 and 6.

CHICKEN SURPRISE

The sauce includes the unusual ingredient, nutmeg. If you have fresh rosemary or thyme on hand, it will taste even better; just triple the amount of dried.

1 chicken, quartered, or 4 favorite
   pieces (breast or leg quarters)
salt and freshly ground pepper to taste
2 tbs. butter
2 tbs. flour
2 cups chicken broth

2 tbs. lemon juice
1/4 cup dry white wine
1/8 tsp. cayenne pepper
1/4 tsp. nutmeg
1/4 tsp. dried rosemary
1/4 tsp. dried savory

Season chicken with salt and pepper. In a large skillet over medium heat, melt butter. Brown chicken on both sides. Remove and set aside.

Reduce heat to medium-low and add flour, distributing evenly over pan; blend flour and butter. Add broth, stirring vigorously and blending. Simmer for 10 minutes, reducing heat further if necessary so that mixture is just simmering. Add lemon juice and wine; add herbs and spices.

Return chicken to pan with any juices that have accumulated. Cover pan. Cook for 40 minutes, or until chicken tests done.

Freeze in plastic freezer bags.

To reheat on the stovetop or in the microwave, see pages 5 and 6.

CHICKEN WITH SALSA AND CORN

Servings: 4

This Mexican-style recipe is tasty and particularly easy to prepare.

2 tbs. canola oil or other oil
4 boneless, skinless chicken breast halves
1 jar (16 oz.) salsa
1 tbs. dark brown sugar
4 thin slices lime
$\frac{1}{2}$ tsp. ground coriander
$\frac{1}{2}$ tsp. ground cumin
$\frac{1}{2}$ tsp. dried oregano
1 can (11 oz.) corn kernels

In a large skillet, heat oil over medium heat. Brown chicken very lightly on both sides. Pour off excess oil and reduce heat to medium-low.

Add salsa to skillet; add sugar, mixing well. Add coriander, cumin and oregano and mix. Add lime slices to sauce.

Cover and cook for 10 minutes. Add corn and mix into sauce. Return lid to skillet and cook for 10 minutes, or until chicken tests done.

Freeze in containers.

To reheat on the stovetop or in the microwave, see pages 5 and 6.

MAPLE CHICKEN

This slightly unusual-tasting chicken is somewhat sweet.

½ cup chicken broth
½ cup dry white wine
3 tbs. maple syrup
1 tbs. soy sauce
3 tbs. red wine vinegar
1 tbs. capers
1 tsp. dried oregano
1 tsp. dried thyme

1 tsp. dried rosemary
1 bay leaf
salt and freshly ground pepper to taste
3 cloves garlic, minced
8 pitted prunes
8 figs, dried or fresh
4 boneless, skinless chicken breast
  halves or turkey cutlets

Combine all ingredients, except chicken, in a large bowl or plastic bag, and add chicken. Cover bowl or seal bag and marinate in the refrigerator for at least 2 hours, turning a few times.

Heat oven to 350°. Place chicken in a large baking pan, pour marinade over chicken and cover pan with aluminum foil. Bake at 350° for 25 minutes. Remove foil, set oven temperature to 400° and cook for 10 minutes. Remove bay leaf.

Freeze in containers.

To reheat on the stovetop or in the microwave, see pages 5 and 6.

PARMESAN CHICKEN WITH CAPERS

The Parmesan cheese, garlic and capers add plenty of zing, without being peppery.

2 tsp. olive oil
4 boneless, skinless chicken breast
    halves
3 cloves garlic, minced

½ cup dry white wine
4 tsp. capers
freshly ground pepper to taste
⅔ cup grated Parmesan cheese

In a large, preferably nonstick skillet, heat oil. Add chicken and cook until lightly browned on both sides. Add garlic and cook for just 10 seconds.

Add wine, capers and pepper. Reduce heat, cover skillet and simmer for 15 minutes, or until chicken tests done. Sprinkle cheese over chicken pieces, distributing evenly, and cover pan for about 1 minute, until cheese is melted.

Freeze each piece of chicken in a microwave-safe single-serving container, rather than a plastic freezer bag, being sure to keep it upright until cheese cools.

Reheat in a microwave in the container, just long enough to warm the chicken through.

GARLICKY CHICKEN

Don't be alarmed at the quantity of garlic. By the time it's finished cooking, this dish is flavorful but no longer sharp.

2 tbs. olive oil or other oil
4 boneless, skinless chicken breast
   halves
1½ cups chicken broth
3 tbs. red wine vinegar

½ tsp. dried sage
½ tsp. dried thyme
¼ tsp. ground ginger
1 cup whole peeled garlic cloves

Heat oven to 400°. In a large skillet, heat oil over medium heat. Add chicken to skillet and cook until lightly browned on both sides. Remove chicken and set aside. Discard oil and add broth and vinegar to skillet. Add sage, thyme and ginger and stir. Raise heat to medium-high and cook for about 2 minutes.

Place garlic cloves in a baking dish or casserole. Place chicken on top of garlic and add any juices that have accumulated. Pour broth mixture over chicken. Cover baking dish or casserole and bake for about 20 minutes.

Remove chicken and keep warm. Pour liquid and garlic into blender. Puree and use as sauce over chicken.

Freeze in containers or plastic bags.

To reheat on the stovetop or in the microwave, see pages 5 and 6.

FLORIDA CITRUS CHICKEN

I got this recipe from a friend in Virginia and changed it somewhat. Add honey to counterbalance the tartness of the citrus; add garlic and hot pepper sauce for the added zing. Voila! You've got Florida Citrus Chicken.

1 chicken, quartered, or 4 favorite pieces (leg or breast quarters)
1/2 cup lemon juice
1/2 cup lime juice
1/2 cup orange juice, or 1/4 cup frozen orange juice concentrate
1/4 cup honey
3 cloves garlic, quartered
1 tbs. hot pepper sauce, such as Tabasco Sauce

Pierce chicken pieces all over with the tines of a fork. Combine all remaining ingredients in a 1-gallon sealable plastic bag. Add chicken and seal bag tightly. Marinate in the refrigerator for 2 hours.

Heat oven to 350°. Bake in 1/2 of the marinade for 30 minutes, or until chicken tests done. Or remove chicken from marinade and grill. If cooked in marinade, remove from marinade before serving.

Freeze in containers or plastic freezer bags.

To reheat on the stovetop or in the microwave, see pages 5 and 6.

CHICKEN WITH MARMALADE

Servings: 4

Here's chicken with a tart-sweet flavor, marrying marmalade, soy sauce, orange juice and garlic.

4 boneless, skinless chicken breast
    halves or turkey cutlets
4 cloves garlic, minced
1/4 cup soy sauce

1 tsp. dried rosemary
1/4 cup orange marmalade
pepper to taste
1/2 cup orange juice

Place chicken pieces in a glass baking dish or casserole. Rub 1 clove of the minced garlic into each piece, leaving garlic on top of chicken after rubbing. Splash 1 tbs. of the soy sauce on each piece. Sprinkle rosemary on each, and top with 1 tbs. marmalade. Sprinkle pepper over all and leave covered in the refrigerator for at least 2 hours.

Heat oven to 350°. Pour orange juice into baking dish and cover. Bake for 20 to 30 minutes or until chicken tests done. Do not turn pieces over while they cook.

Freeze in plastic containers.

This reheats best if kept in the same flat position. Reheat in one layer in a covered skillet or in a microwave at 70% power. To reheat on the stovetop or in the microwave, see pages 5 and 6. Do not overcook or meat will toughen.

CHINESE BARBECUE-STYLE CHICKEN

Servings: 4

It's not truly barbecued, or truly Chinese, but it's good, and easy to make. Hoisin sauce can be found in the Asian foods section of your supermarket.

1/2 cup hoisin sauce
3 tbs. soy sauce
3 tbs. rice wine or sake, or white wine
1 1/2 tbs. brown sugar
2 tbs. ketchup

2 tbs. minced garlic
2 tsp. ground ginger
3 green onions, white part only, thinly sliced
1 chicken, quartered

Combine all ingredients except chicken into a marinade, mixing well. Put chicken into a covered bowl or plastic bag with marinade, being sure marinade completely covers chicken. Marinate in the refrigerator for at least 1 hour, and preferably overnight.

Heat oven to 375°. Remove chicken from marinade and place skin-side down in a shallow roasting pan or on a foil-lined rimmed cookie sheet. Bake for 20 minutes and turn skin-side up. Bake for an additional 30 minutes or until thoroughly cooked.

To freeze, wrap each piece well in aluminum foil.

To reheat on the stovetop or in the microwave, see pages 5 and 6.

TIJUANA CHICKEN

Servings: 4

This bona fide fraud was conceived well north of the border, but is full of hearty Mexican flavors.

1 tbs. canola oil
4 boneless, skinless chicken breast halves
salt and freshly ground pepper to taste
1 large onion, sliced
4 cloves garlic, sliced
1 can (14.5 oz.) diced tomatoes, with juice
1 can (15 oz.) ready-to-eat Cuban-style black beans, such as Goya brand

1 can (11–15 oz.) corn kernels
1 can (4.5 oz.) chopped green chiles, drained
2 tbs. lime juice
$1/2$ cup chopped green olives, stuffed or unstuffed
1 jar (6.5 oz.) pimientos, drained and coarsely chopped

Heat oil in large skillet over medium heat. Season chicken with salt and pepper. Cook onion and garlic until wilted but not brown. Add chicken and cook for 4 to 6 minutes a side, until lightly browned. Add all remaining ingredients and simmer for 15 minutes, or until chicken is cooked through. Cut into center to test for doneness.

Freeze in containers.

To reheat on the stovetop or in the microwave, see pages 5 and 6.

SPANISH-STYLE CHICKEN WITH PRUNES

Spanish flavors combine with prunes to make an unusual dish, worthy of company — good, different, impressive, special.

4 cloves garlic, pressed
2 tbs. dried oregano
salt and freshly ground pepper to taste
$\frac{1}{2}$ cup red wine vinegar
$\frac{1}{2}$ cup olive oil
1 cup pitted prunes
$\frac{1}{2}$ cup stuffed green olives
$\frac{1}{2}$ cup capers, with several drops caper brine
4 bay leaves
6 chicken breast halves, with or without bones and
    skin
1 cup dry white wine
1 cup brown sugar, packed

Combine garlic, oregano, salt, pepper, vinegar, oil, prunes, olives, capers, brine and bay leaves. Mix well and add chicken, coating well. Cover and marinate in the refrigerator for at least 6 hours.

Heat oven to 350°. Place chicken in a baking pan large enough to hold chicken in a single layer. Mix wine with marinade and pour evenly over chicken. Sprinkle brown sugar over each chicken piece. Bake breasts with bones for 50 minutes to 1 hour, or boneless breasts for about 40 minutes, or until chicken tests done. Remove bay leaves.

Freeze sugar-side up in containers.

Reheat in a 325° oven in a baking dish or small roasting pan covered tightly with aluminum foil. Allow about 20 to 25 minutes for boneless breasts or about 45 to 50 minutes for breasts with bones.

SPICY SOUTHWESTERN CHICKEN

In the Southwest, the Mexican influence shows up in everything from food to clothing and home decoration. This recipe has many of the traditional ingredients.

1 tbs. chili powder
1¼ tsp. ground cumin
salt to taste
¼ tsp. cayenne pepper
½ tsp. dried oregano
4 boneless, skinless chicken breast halves
2 tsp. olive oil
½ cup chicken broth
1 tbs. cider vinegar
8 oz. ripe plum tomatoes, diced
1 can (11 oz.) corn kernels
1 can (4.5 oz.) chopped green chiles, drained
¼ cup chopped fresh cilantro
1 lime, sliced

In a small bowl, mix chili powder, cumin, salt, cayenne and oregano. Use 1 rounded tablespoon of this spice mixture to rub both sides of chicken breasts. Reserve remaining spice mixture.

In a large skillet, heat oil over medium heat. Add chicken and cook just until spice coating has browned on both sides and surface is opaque. Remove chicken and set aside.

Add broth, vinegar and reserved spice mixture to skillet. Increase heat and bring mixture to a boil. Scrape up browned bits from the bottom of the skillet and boil for 2 minutes.

Return chicken to skillet with any juices that have accumulated. Add tomatoes, corn and chiles. Mix well, cover and simmer for 10 minutes, or until chicken tests done. Remove from heat and add cilantro and lime.

Freeze in containers.

Reheat in a 325° oven in a baking dish or roasting pan covered tightly with aluminum foil. Heat for about 20 to 25 minutes. Or to reheat on the stovetop or in the microwave, see pages 5 and 6.

CHICKEN ABLAZE

Servings: 4

So named for its peppery punch. You are free to adjust the heat to suit your taste.

2 tbs. canola oil or other oil
1 chicken, quartered, or 4 favorite
 pieces (breast or leg quarters)
1 cup chopped celery
2 cups chopped onion
1 green bell pepper, diced

2 cups tomato juice
6 tbs. cider vinegar
salt and freshly ground pepper to taste
$3/4$ tsp. hot pepper sauce, such as
 Tabasco Sauce, or to taste

Heat oven to 350°. In a large skillet, heat oil over medium heat. When oil is hot, add chicken and cook until browned. Remove and place in a baking dish large enough to hold pieces in one layer.

Add celery, onion and green pepper to skillet and cook until wilted. Add remaining ingredients to skillet and bring to a boil. Simmer for 2 minutes and pour over chicken in baking dish. Bake uncovered for 40 to 50 minutes, until thoroughly cooked, basting 2 or 3 times during cooking.

Freeze in plastic freezer bags.

Reheat in a 325° oven in a baking dish or small roasting pan covered tightly with aluminum foil for about 35 minutes.

CHICKEN BREASTS WITH MUSTARD SAUCE

Servings: 4

The mustard sauce makes this a rich and delicious main course.

1 tbs. butter
4 boneless, skinless chicken breast
  halves
salt and freshly ground pepper to taste
1 small onion, minced
1/4 tsp. dried thyme

1 tbs. red wine vinegar
1/4 cup dry white wine
1/2 cup chicken broth
2 tsp. tomato paste
1/4 cup heavy cream
1 tbs. Dijon mustard

Heat butter in a large skillet over medium heat. Sprinkle chicken breasts with salt and pepper. Add breasts to skillet and cook on each side until starting to brown. Remove and set aside.

Add onion and thyme to skillet, cooking just until onion is wilted. Add vinegar and wine and bring to a medium boil. Add stock and tomato paste, stirring tomato paste well into mixture, and cook at a medium boil for about 7 minutes.

While sauce cooks, cut chicken into bite-sized pieces. After 7 minutes, add cream and mustard, stirring with each addition. Reduce heat, return chicken to skillet and coat with sauce. Simmer for 3 minutes.

Freeze in containers.

To reheat on the stovetop or in the microwave, see pages 5 and 6.

CHICKEN CURRY

Adjust the amount of curry powder to your taste. If you buy chicken precut for stir-fry, you will save some time. This curry is good with rice and broccoli.

2 containers (8 oz. each) plain yogurt
1–1 1/2 tbs. curry powder, or to taste
2 tbs. chopped fresh basil
4 boneless, skinless chicken breast
    halves or turkey cutlets, cut into strips

flour to coat chicken
1 red onion, cut into strips
1 green bell pepper, cut into strips
1 red bell pepper, cut into strips
2 tbs. vegetable oil

Mix yogurt, curry powder and basil together in a bowl. Cover and refrigerate for a few minutes to blend flavors.

Toss chicken strips in flour to coat. Heat oil in a large skillet or wok over high heat. When it begins to smoke, brown chicken strips in small batches to keep oil from cooling. Stir constantly. As they brown, remove and set aside. Add onion and peppers to pan. Stir until wilted and onion begins to turn golden.

Return chicken to pan and add yogurt mixture. Reduce heat to medium-low, stir contents of pan well and cook for about 5 minutes. When chicken is cooked through and sauce has thickened, the dish is done.

Freeze in containers or plastic freezer bags.

To reheat on the stovetop or in the microwave, see pages 5 and 6.

CHICKEN WITH ARTICHOKES

This is another chicken dish that's elegant enough for guests.

3 tbs. olive oil
4 boneless, skinless chicken breast
   halves, cut into 2-inch-square pieces
2 cloves garlic, finely chopped
$1/2$ lb. mushrooms, sliced
4 thin lemon slices
1 tbs. flour

salt and freshly ground pepper to taste
$1/2$ tsp. dried oregano
$1/4$ tsp. dried thyme
$1/4$ tsp. dried savory
$1/2$ cup dry white wine
1 can (14 oz.) unmarinated artichoke
   hearts, drained and quartered

Heat oil in a large skillet over medium heat until hot. Add chicken and cook, turning, until opaque on all sides. Remove and set aside.

Add garlic, mushrooms and lemon slices to skillet. Cook until mushrooms are tender and have changed color. Sprinkle flour and seasonings into skillet and cook for 1 minute, stirring.

Add wine and bring to a boil, stirring. When mixture thickens, add artichoke hearts and chicken. Reduce heat and simmer until chicken tests done.

Freeze in containers.

To reheat on the stovetop or in the microwave, see pages 5 and 6.

CHICKEN ARRABBIATO

"Arrabbiato" means "angry", and refers to the red pepper in the recipe.

1 pkg. (1 oz.) dried, imported mushrooms
1 chicken, quartered, or 4 favorite pieces (breast
   or leg quarters)
salt and freshly ground pepper to taste
2 cups canned tomatoes, with juice
3 tbs. olive oil
12 thin slices hard salami, cut into matchstick
   strips
3 cloves garlic, finely chopped
½ cup dry white wine
1 tsp. red pepper flakes

Reconstitute dried mushrooms for about 1 hour in a bowl with enough warm water to cover.

Season chicken with salt and pepper. In a saucepan, cook tomatoes until reduced to 1 cup. Heat oil in a large skillet over medium heat. Add chicken to skillet skin-side down, and brown. Turn over to brown second side. While browning, add salami strips, stirring to brown lightly. When browned, remove and set aside.

Pour fat from skillet and add garlic. Cook until wilted but not brown, and add wine. Reduce heat and simmer until reduced by half; add tomatoes.

Squeeze mushrooms to remove excess liquid; reserve ½ cup mushroom liquid. Add mushrooms to skillet with reserved liquid. Add red pepper flakes and additional salt and pepper if desired. Return chicken and salami to sauce and cook until chicken tests done.

Freeze in plastic freezer bags.

Reheat in a 325° oven in a baking dish or roasting pan covered tightly with aluminum foil for about 40 minutes.

JAMAICAN SWEET CHICKEN

Servings: 4

This dish has a hint of sweetness from vermouth, a hint of sharpness from Dijon mustard and citrus juices, and a taste very different from anything you've had before. Serve it with rice to sop up the sauce.

1/2 cup dry white wine
1/4 cup sweet vermouth
1/4 cup lime juice
1/4 cup lemon juice
1/4 cup Worcestershire sauce
4 tbs. Dijon mustard, divided
1/4 tsp. ground cumin
1 tsp. Old Bay seasoning
1/4 tsp. freshly ground pepper
1/4 tsp. dried thyme
1/4 tsp. dried basil
1/4 tsp. dried tarragon
1/4 tsp. dried savory
4 boneless, skinless chicken breast halves
1 1/2 tbs. butter

In a large bowl, combine wine, vermouth, citrus juices, Worcestershire sauce, 2 tbs. of the mustard and seasonings. Blend well, add chicken and marinate in a covered bowl or a sealed plastic bag in the refrigerator for at least 1 hour.

Heat oven to 350°. Remove chicken from marinade and place in a baking dish large enough to hold chicken in one layer. Reserve marinade. Rub chicken breasts with butter and remaining mustard. Pour reserved marinade over chicken breasts. Cover dish and bake for 45 minutes. Serve cooked marinade with chicken.

Freeze in containers or plastic freezer bags.

Reheat in a 325° oven in a baking dish or roasting pan covered tightly with aluminum foil. Heat for about 40 minutes.

CHICKEN KORMA

Korma is a spicy curry dish from India or Pakistan. Here's a variation for chicken that's easy to cook. The results are delicious. Serve it with rice and a vegetable of your choice.

2 cups plain yogurt
8 tsp. curry powder, or to taste
2 tsp. salt
2 tsp. ground coriander
2 tsp. minced fresh ginger
8 cloves garlic, minced
1 tsp. cayenne pepper or red pepper flakes, or to taste
1 tsp. lemon juice
4 boneless, skinless chicken breast halves
1 tbs. canola oil
1 medium onion, chopped
1 large tomato, peeled and chopped
2 bay leaves

In a large bowl, combine yogurt, curry powder, salt, coriander, ginger, garlic, red pepper and lemon juice. Stir well, add chicken and stir again to coat well. Cover bowl and marinate in the refrigerator for at least 1 hour; longer is better.

Heat oil in a large skillet over medium heat. Add onion and cook until lightly browned. Stir in tomato and bay leaves and cook for 5 minutes. Add chicken and marinade and mix well. Reduce heat, cover and simmer for about 30 minutes, stirring occasionally. Remove bay leaves.

Freeze in containers.

To reheat on the stovetop or in the microwave, see pages 5 and 6. On the stovetop, use a skillet and check frequently to avoid burning or drying sauce.

CHICKEN ESPAÑA WITH CREAM

Servings: 4

Cream, sherry and fresh ginger combine to make a scrumptious sauce for this chicken. It will be even better if you have fresh herbs on hand; use triple the amount of dried.

salt and freshly ground pepper to taste
4 boneless, skinless chicken breast
   halves
2 tbs. butter
1/2 cup orange juice
1/2 cup heavy cream

1 tbs. sherry
3/4 tsp. grated fresh ginger
1/2 tsp. dried thyme
1/2 tsp. dried oregano
1/2 tsp. dried rosemary

Salt and pepper chicken. Heat butter in a large skillet over medium heat. Brown chicken lightly on both sides.

Mix orange juice, cream, sherry, ginger and herbs in a bowl. When chicken is lightly browned on both sides, reduce heat to medium-low and add orange juice mixture to skillet. Cook for about 20 minutes, or until chicken tests done.

Freeze in containers.

To reheat on the stovetop or in the microwave, see pages 5 and 6.

CREAMY TARRAGON CHICKEN

Servings: 4

Richly flavored cream sauce is simple to make with tarragon and Dijon mustard.

3 tbs. canola oil or other oil
4 boneless, skinless chicken breast halves
1 cup dry white wine
1 tbs. Dijon mustard
1 tsp. dried tarragon
1/2 tsp. dried thyme
salt and freshly ground pepper to taste
1 cup heavy cream

In a large skillet, heat oil over medium heat. Add chicken and brown lightly on both sides. Remove chicken from skillet and set aside. Drain oil from skillet.

To same skillet, add wine and bring to a boil. Add mustard, herbs, salt and pepper and stir. Add cream, whisking it in, and boil gently for a few minutes until mixture thickens. Reduce heat, add browned chicken, coat with sauce and simmer for about 15 minutes.

Freeze in containers.

To reheat on the stovetop or in the microwave, see pages 5 and 6.

EASY CHICKEN IN WHITE WINE

Servings: 4

This easy chicken dish produces delicious aromas, both when you first cook it and when you reheat it.

4 boneless, skinless chicken breast halves
salt and freshly ground pepper to taste
1 tbs. canola oil or other oil
1 tbs. butter or margarine
6 cloves garlic, sliced
1/2 tsp. dried rosemary, crushed
1/2 tsp. dried thyme
1/4 tsp. dried tarragon
1/4 cup dry white wine
1/4 cup chicken broth

Season chicken with salt and pepper. Heat oil and butter in a large skillet over medium heat. Add garlic cloves, cooking only until slightly wilted.

Add chicken and cook until lightly browned on both sides. Add remaining ingredients and cook for about 20 minutes, turning chicken once.

Freeze in containers.

To reheat on the stovetop or in the microwave, see pages 5 and 6.

INDONESIAN CHICKEN BREASTS
WITH PEANUT BUTTER SAUCE

Servings: 4

Exotic flavors come from common ingredients. Serve this dish with hot rice.

1 cup orange juice
1/2 cup smooth peanut butter, prefer no additives
4 tsp. curry powder
4 boneless, skinless chicken breast halves
1 red bell pepper, cut into strips
1/4 cup shredded coconut
1/4 cup dried currants

Combine orange juice, peanut butter and curry powder in a non-metal bowl. Blend thoroughly. Add chicken and coat well. Cover bowl and refrigerate for at least 1 hour, or up to 1 day.

Heat oven to 350°. Place chicken and marinade in a baking dish large enough to hold all 4 pieces in one layer and add pepper strips. Bake for 30 minutes. Remove from oven and add coconut and currants.

Freeze in containers.

To reheat on the stovetop or in the microwave, see pages 5 and 6.

CHICKEN PAPRIKA

Paprika combines with lemon, garlic, rosemary and cayenne pepper to give this chicken dish oomph.

3 tbs. olive oil
5 cloves garlic, minced
juice and zest of 1 lemon
4 boneless, skinless chicken breast
   halves
salt and freshly ground pepper to taste

1 tbs. plus 1 tsp. chopped fresh rosemary
1 tsp. dried thyme
$1/4$ cup paprika
cayenne pepper to taste
2 cups chicken broth

Heat oven to 350°. Heat oil in a medium skillet over medium heat. Sauté garlic until wilted. Add lemon juice and zest and cook for 2 minutes.

Season chicken with salt and pepper and place in a baking dish large enough to hold all 4 pieces of chicken in one layer. Sprinkle with rosemary, thyme, paprika and cayenne. Pour oil-garlic-lemon mixture over chicken and add chicken broth. Cover with aluminum foil and bake for 15 minutes. Uncover and bake for 15 minutes.

Freeze in containers.

Reheat in a 350° oven in a baking dish in one layer. Cover tightly with aluminum foil and heat for about 40 minutes.

CHILI CHICKEN

If you love the flavor of chili; if you prefer chicken to beef; if you're tired of the same old chili; or if you're just looking for a new twist on chicken — this recipe is right up your alley.

2 tbs. canola oil or other oil
2 onions, chopped
1 can (14.5 oz.) diced tomatoes, with juice
6 tsp. chili powder, divided

1 tsp. dried oregano
$1/2$ tsp. ground cumin
4 boneless, skinless chicken breast halves or turkey cutlets
salt to taste

Heat oven to 350°. Heat oil in a medium skillet over medium heat and cook onions until translucent. Transfer to a baking dish large enough to hold chicken pieces in one layer, and add tomatoes, 4 tsp. of the chili powder, oregano and cumin. Mix well.

Sprinkle chicken with salt and remaining 2 tsp. chili powder, and rub into chicken. Place chicken pieces on top of tomato mixture. Bake uncovered about 30 minutes, or until chicken tests done.

Freeze in containers or plastic freezer bags.

Reheat in a 350° oven in a baking dish covered tightly with aluminum foil for about 35 minutes, or reheat on the stovetop or in the microwave; see pages 5 and 6.

BAKED CHICKEN IN BARBEQUE SAUCE

Servings: 4

The flavors of grilled chicken are possible even without the grill when you cook it in this barbecue sauce.

4 boneless, skinless chicken breast halves
1/2 cup ketchup
1/2 cup vegetable oil
1/2 cup cider vinegar
2 tbs. Worcestershire sauce
4 drops Tabasco Sauce

1/2 cup brown sugar, packed
2 heaping tsp. Dijon mustard
1 tsp. ground ginger
2 cloves garlic, pressed
juice of 1 medium lemon
salt and freshly ground pepper to taste

Heat oven to 350°. Place chicken breast halves in a baking dish large enough to hold all 4 pieces in one layer.

In a saucepan, combine all remaining ingredients and stir well. Bring to a boil, pour over chicken and bake for about 30 minutes, or until thickest part of largest piece of chicken tests done.

Freeze in containers or plastic freezer bags.

Reheat in a 325° oven in a baking pan or roasting pan covered tightly with aluminum foil for about 35 minutes. Or reheat on the stovetop or in the microwave; see pages 5 and 6.

PICKLED CHICKEN

Pickling spices mix with tomatoes, honey, soy sauce, onions and garlic for a flavor that's unusually good.

¹/₂ cup pickling spices
3 medium onions, peeled and halved
5 cloves garlic, peeled and halved
1 chicken, quartered, or 4 favorite pieces (breast or leg quarters)
¹/₄ cup soy sauce
¹/₄ cup honey
1 can (14.5 oz.) whole tomatoes, with juice
1 can (12 oz.) tomato paste
2 cans (15 oz. each) tomato sauce
1 cup red wine

In a Dutch oven or large pot, place pickling spices, onions and garlic. Layer chicken pieces on top and add remaining ingredients. Bring to a boil, reduce heat, cover and simmer for 1 hour.

Freeze in plastic freezer bags.

To reheat on the stovetop or in the microwave, see pages 5 and 6.

CHICKEN IN DIJON MUSHROOM SAUCE

Servings: 4

This recipe makes a rich, thick, flavorful sauce that goes well with rice or barley. The reconstituted mushrooms augment the mushroom soup that forms the base for the sauce, and the capers give it zing.

1 pkg. (1 oz.) dried imported mushrooms
2 tbs. canola oil or other oil
1 tbs. butter
4 boneless, skinless chicken breast halves
3 cloves garlic, diced
2 onions, diced
1/2 cup sherry
2 cans (10.75 oz. each) cream of mushroom soup, undiluted
1 tbs. plus 1 tsp. Dijon mustard
2 tsp. Worcestershire sauce
2 tsp. paprika
1/4 cup chopped fresh dill
1 tsp. dried sage
2 tsp. capers, drained

Reconstitute mushrooms for 1 hour in a bowl with enough warm water to cover.

Heat oil and butter in a large skillet over medium heat. Add chicken, garlic and onions and cook until chicken is lightly browned on both sides. Squeeze excess water out of mushrooms and add to skillet.

Reduce heat to medium-low and add remaining ingredients. Cover and cook for 15 to 20 minutes more, or until chicken tests done. Turn once during cooking.

Freeze in containers or in plastic freezer bags.

To reheat on the stovetop or in the microwave, see pages 5 and 6.

EAST MEETS WEST CHICKEN

Servings: 4

If you store ginger in a covered jar in white vermouth or vodka, it will keep forever, and you will always have "fresh" ginger available for cooking.

2 tbs. peanut oil or other oil
1 chicken quartered, or 4 favorite
   pieces (breast or leg quarters)
1/4 cup grated fresh ginger
4 green onions, white and green parts,
   thinly sliced
4 cloves garlic, thinly sliced

juice of 1/2 lime
1/4 cup soy sauce
1 cup chicken broth
1/2 tsp. nutmeg
1 can (8 oz.) Chinese baby corn,
   drained
1 can (7 oz.) sliced water chestnuts

Heat oil in a large skillet over medium heat. Add chicken, skin-side down. In a bowl, combine ginger, green onions, garlic, lime juice, soy sauce, chicken broth and nutmeg.

When chicken is browned, pour broth mixture over chicken and reduce heat to medium-low. Cover skillet and cook for about 40 minutes, turning chicken over after about 30 minutes. Add corn and water chestnuts about 5 minutes before end of cooking time.

Freeze in plastic freezer bags.

To reheat on the stovetop or in the microwave, see pages 5 and 6.

CHICKEN PRESTO

One or two preparations, and PRESTO! You have dinner. The marinade does most of the work.

½ cup smooth peanut butter, prefer no additives

8 oz. yogurt

2 tsp. brown sugar

¼ cup grated fresh ginger

3 cloves garlic, finely chopped

4 green onions, white and green parts, thinly sliced

1 tsp. hot paprika

1 tsp. cayenne pepper

1 tsp. ground cumin

1 tsp. dried turmeric

juice of ½ lime

1 chicken, quartered, or 4 favorite pieces (breast or leg quarters)

In a bowl, mix all ingredients, except chicken. Blend well to incorporate peanut butter. Add chicken and marinate in the refrigerator for at least 3 hours.

Heat oven to 350°. Put chicken in a baking pan with marinade and cover with aluminum foil. Bake for 15 minutes. Uncover and bake for an additional 30 minutes.

Freeze in plastic freezer bags.

To reheat on the stovetop or in the microwave, see pages 5 and 6.

CHICKEN AND TURKEY   55

CHEESY CHICKEN WITH ARTICHOKES

Servings: 4

Parmesan cheese adds a slightly salty sharp flavor to this dish. The evaporated skim milk keeps down the calories.

2 cups chicken broth
4 boneless, skinless chicken breast halves
2 tbs. olive oil
1 medium onion, finely chopped
2 cloves garlic, sliced
3/4 cup evaporated skim milk
2 tbs. cornstarch
2 tbs. dry white wine
1/3 cup grated Parmesan cheese
1/2 tsp. dried rosemary
salt and freshly ground white pepper to taste
1 can (14 oz.) unmarinated artichoke hearts, drained and quartered, 1/4 cup
    liquid reserved
1/2 lb. mushrooms, sliced

In a large skillet, heat broth, adding chicken when broth begins to simmer. Simmer, covered, for 10 to 15 minutes, or until chicken no longer shows any pink when tested. Reserve 3/4 cup of the broth and discard the rest. Cut chicken into bite-sized pieces and set aside.

In a medium saucepan, heat oil over medium heat. Add onion and garlic. When onion is translucent and wilted, stir in reserved stock and milk.

In a bowl, mix cornstarch with wine until smooth. Add cornstarch-wine mixture to broth-milk mixture in saucepan. Stir and bring to a boil. Reduce heat to simmer. Continue to stir intermittently and cook for 1 minute. Stir in Parmesan cheese, rosemary, salt and pepper. Continue cooking until cheese is fully melted.

Heat oven to 350°. Lightly spray a 2-quart casserole with nonstick spray. Arrange chicken in casserole. Add artichoke quarters, distributing evenly. Pour cheese sauce over all. Cover and bake for 30 minutes.

While chicken bakes, heat reserved artichoke liquid in a medium skillet over medium heat. Add mushrooms and cook, stirring occasionally, until mushrooms are soft and tender. When casserole is done, top with mushrooms.

Freeze in containers.

Reheat on the stovetop over medium-low heat; see pages 5 and 6.

CHICKEN ITALIAN-STYLE (PETTI DI POLLO)

Servings: 4

Chicken Italian-style adds to your store of chicken flavors from many cultures.

4 boneless, skinless chicken breast halves
salt and freshly ground pepper to taste
flour
3 tbs. butter or margarine
2 tbs. olive oil
8 thin slices prosciutto
8 thin slices fontina or Bel Paese cheese
4 tsp. grated Parmesan cheese

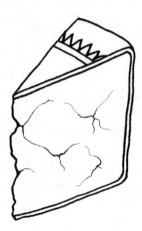

Heat oven to 325°. Cut each chicken breast half into 2 pieces across its width to make 8 pieces. Pound pieces to about ¼-inch thickness (or buy thinly sliced chicken breasts and omit the pounding) between layers of waxed paper or plastic wrap with a meat mallet or heavy pan. Add salt, pepper and a dusting of flour to each chicken piece. Shake off excess flour.

Heat oil and butter in a large skillet over medium heat. Add chicken pieces and cook until lightly golden. As pieces are ready, transfer them to a flat baking dish or pan large enough to hold all 8 pieces in one layer.

On top of each, place a slice of prosciutto topped with a slice of cheese. Sprinkle all with Parmesan and bake, uncovered, for about 10 minutes, or until both cheeses are melted and very lightly browned.

Wrap each piece of chicken, with its prosciutto and cheese, in plastic wrap and then in aluminum foil, and freeze.

To reheat, lightly spray a baking dish or pan with nonstick cooking spray. Remove wrapping from chicken, place in pan and heat in a 325° oven for about 25 minutes.

HONEY GARLIC CHICKEN

Servings: 4

A little sweet and a little sharp, this recipe offers the yin and yang — honey and garlic — of sauce for chicken.

2 tbs. olive oil or other oil
4 boneless, skinless chicken breast halves
1/2 cup chicken broth
1/4 cup honey
1/4 cup soy sauce
2 tbs. ketchup
3 cloves garlic, minced

Heat oil in a large skillet over medium heat. Add chicken and cook until lightly browned on both sides.

Heat broth in a saucepan over medium heat. When broth simmers, turn off heat and add remaining ingredients, stirring vigorously and blending well.

Drain any fat from skillet and pour sauce over chicken in skillet. Reduce heat, cover and simmer for about 25 minutes.

Freeze in containers or plastic freezer bags.

To reheat on the stovetop or in the microwave, see pages 5 and 6.

CHICKEN WITH YOGURT AND MUSTARD

Servings: 4

Chicken and mushrooms nestle in a speckled sauce that goes well with noodles, barley or rice. It's an easy recipe to prepare, and it's good for those of you who are watching your weight, too.

3 tbs. butter or margarine
1/2 lb. mushrooms, sliced
2 containers (8 oz. each) plain yogurt, can be nonfat
2 tbs. Dijon mustard
salt and freshly ground pepper to taste
1/2 tsp. dried thyme
4 boneless, skinless chicken breast halves or turkey cutlets

Heat oven to 400°. In a medium or large skillet, heat butter over medium heat. Add mushrooms and sauté until golden.

In a baking dish large enough to hold chicken pieces in one layer, mix yogurt, mustard, salt, pepper and thyme. Add chicken, turning to coat well. When mushrooms are ready, drain and add to chicken and sauce. Bake for 45 minutes.

Freeze in containers or plastic freezer bags.

To reheat on the stovetop or in the microwave, see pages 5 and 6.

CHICKEN AND RICE SKILLET DINNER

Here is your entire dinner in one package, simple and delicious.

6 boneless, skinless chicken breast halves, cut into bite-sized pieces
salt and freshly ground pepper to taste
2 tbs. vegetable oil
1 green or red bell pepper, diced
2 carrots, thinly sliced
1 cup sliced celery
4 onions, chopped
6 cloves garlic, chopped
2 cans (14.5 oz. each) diced tomatoes, with juice
1 cup chicken broth
1 cup pitted black olives
$1/2$ tsp. dried rosemary
$1/2$ tsp. dried savory
$1/2$ tsp. dried thyme
$1/2$ tsp. ground cumin
1 cup uncooked rice

Season chicken with salt and pepper. Heat oil in a large skillet over medium heat. Add chicken and cook until no pink shows. Add pepper, carrots, celery, onions and garlic and cook all until onions and garlic are soft but not brown.

Add tomatoes with their juice, broth, olives, herbs and cumin. Stir in rice, bring to a boil, reduce heat, cover and simmer for about 25 minutes. Stir once about halfway through.

Freeze in plastic freezer bags.

To reheat on the stovetop or in the microwave, see pages 5 and 6.

NORTHSIDE CHICKEN WITH BLACK BEANS

Servings: 4

I'm absolutely wild about this chicken, so I named it after the street I live on, which I'm pretty fond of too.

2 pkg. (1 oz. each) dried imported mushrooms
2 tbs. vegetable oil
8 cloves garlic, sliced
4 boneless, skinless chicken breast halves
1 cup chicken broth
3/4 cup dry white wine
juice of 1/2 lime
2 tsp. Dijon mustard
1 can (15 oz.) ready-to-eat Cuban-style black beans, such as Goya brand
1 tbs. grated fresh ginger
1/2 cup sliced, pitted black olives
1 tsp. dried rosemary
paprika and salt to taste

Reconstitute mushrooms by soaking for 1 hour in enough water to cover.

Heat oil over medium heat in a large skillet. Add garlic and cook until soft but not brown. Remove garlic and set aside. Add chicken to skillet and cook until lightly browned on both sides.

Add broth, wine, lime juice and mustard. Mix well. Add beans, ginger and olives. Return garlic to skillet. Squeeze water from mushrooms and add them with rosemary, salt and paprika. Cook for 30 minutes.

Freeze in plastic freezer bags.

To reheat on the stovetop or in the microwave, see pages 5 and 6.

PEANUT CHICKEN

Servings: 3

The flavors of Thai chicken saté are so delicious, I wanted to create something similar in a recipe that would freeze successfully. This is the result.

3 tbs. smooth peanut butter, prefer no additives
3 tbs. plum jam or chutney
2 tbs. water
1 1/2 tsp. lemon juice
1 1/2 tsp. soy sauce
1 tsp. sesame oil
2 tsp. olive oil
1/2 tsp. ground ginger
3 boneless, skinless chicken breast halves, cut into bite-sized pieces
1/4 cup sliced green onion, white part only

Prepare peanut sauce: In a small bowl, blend peanut butter, jam or chutney, water, lemon juice, soy sauce and sesame oil with the back of a spoon until well blended and smooth.

Heat olive oil in a large skillet over medium-high heat. Add ginger to oil and mix well. Add chicken and brown quickly, stirring, until pieces are cooked through. With a slotted spoon, remove chicken and set aside. Drain oil from pan.

Return chicken to pan immediately, add peanut sauce and stir to coat. Mix in green onion.

Freeze in containers.

Reheat food in its container, in the microwave at 50% power. Length of time will depend on your microwave and on how many portions or containers you heat at one time: start with 4 minutes per portion and test often. See pages 5 and 6.

BASIL CHICKEN

Servings: 4

This is very good with fresh basil, but either fresh or dried will work.

4 boneless, skinless chicken breast halves
salt, freshly ground pepper and paprika to taste
2 tbs. canola oil or olive oil
1 clove garlic, sliced
1/2 cup chicken broth
1/2 cup dry white wine
1 tbs. chopped fresh basil, or 1 tsp. dried

Season chicken with salt, pepper and paprika. Heat oil in a large skillet over medium heat. Add chicken and cook for 5 minutes on each side. Two minutes after turning, add garlic slices.

When chicken has been cooked on both sides, add remaining ingredients, bring to a boil, reduce heat, cover and simmer for 10 minutes or until chicken tests done.

Freeze in containers.

To reheat on the stovetop or in the microwave, see pages 5 and 6.

PORTUGUESE CHICKEN

This simple-to-cook, delicious dish will become a family favorite.

3 tbs. butter or margarine
1 chicken, quartered, or 4 favorite
   pieces (leg or breast quarters)
1/2 small onion, finely chopped
1 tbs. flour
1 clove garlic, finely chopped

1/2 cup red wine
1/2 cup chicken broth
1 can (14.5 oz.) diced tomatoes,
   drained
salt and freshly ground pepper to taste

Over medium heat in a large skillet, heat butter. Add chicken, browning well on all sides. Remove chicken and set aside. Add onion to skillet, stirring until translucent and beginning to become golden. Reduce heat to medium-low. Add flour and garlic and stir.

While continuing to stir, slowly add wine and broth. Blend flour well until mixture is smooth and continue to cook until it starts to thicken. Add tomatoes, salt and pepper. Stir.

Return chicken to skillet, cover and adjust heat to simmer. Cook until chicken is tender and thoroughly cooked, about 40 minutes.

Freeze in plastic freezer bags.

To reheat on the stovetop or in the microwave, see pages 5 and 6.

BRUNSWICK STEW

I've seen many recipes for Brunswick stew, most calling for chicken as the main ingredient, but a few calling for meats as exotic as squirrel! In this version, the ingredients are all familiar.

2 tbs. vegetable oil
2 medium onions, thinly sliced
2 cloves garlic, finely chopped
4 turkey cutlets or boneless, skinless chicken breast halves
2 cans (11 oz. each) corn kernels
1 jar pimientos, small or large jar
1 green bell pepper, cut into bite-sized pieces
salt and freshly ground pepper to taste
1 tbs. plus 1 tsp. brown sugar
$1/2$ small lemon, thinly sliced
$3/4$ cup dry sherry
2 bay leaves
6 drops hot pepper sauce, such as Tabasco Sauce
$1/4$ tsp. dried turmeric
1 cup water or chicken or vegetable broth
$3/4$ cup frozen peas, optional

In a medium skillet, heat oil. Add onions and garlic and cook until translucent. Place onions, garlic and all remaining ingredients in a pot large enough to hold them and cook over medium-low heat for about 30 minutes, until turkey is properly cooked and flavors are blended. Remove bay leaves.

Freeze in plastic freezer bags or larger containers.

To reheat on the stovetop or in the microwave, see pages 5 and 6.

BAKED TURKEY FESTA

Servings: 4–5

Chicken and Italian sausage make a happy couple — and the "wedding" is right in your kitchen! You can use mild or hot sausage, according to your taste — I prefer the hot variety.

1 tbs. olive oil or other oil
1 lb. Italian sausage, mild or hot, cut into chunks
3 lb. turkey breast, cut into 4 or 5 serving pieces, or 1 chicken, cut into serving pieces
2 onions, chopped
4 cloves garlic, chopped
1 green bell pepper, diced
1 cup frozen peas
2 cans (15 oz. each) tomato sauce
1/2 cup red wine
3 tbs. tomato paste
1 tbs. Worcestershire sauce
3 drops hot pepper sauce, such as Tabasco Sauce
1 bay leaf
1 tsp. dried basil
1 tsp. dried oregano

Heat oven to 350°. In a large skillet over medium heat, heat oil. Add sausage and chicken and cook until browned.

Add all remaining ingredients to a baking pan large enough to hold chicken and sausage pieces in a single layer. Mix well. As turkey and sausage pieces become browned, transfer them to baking pan. When all pieces are browned, bake for 40 minutes, or until turkey tests done. Remove bay leaf.

Freeze in plastic freezer bags.

To reheat on the stovetop or in the microwave, see pages 5 and 6.

EASY POULTRY À LA KING

This is a great recipe for leftover holiday turkey or cooked chicken. Expand or reduce the recipe according to the amount of cooked poultry available.

2 tbs. butter or margarine
1 lb. mushrooms, sliced
2 cans (10.75 oz. each) cream of mushroom soup, undiluted
1 cup sherry
1 cup frozen peas
1 medium onion, minced
1 green bell pepper, diced
1 carrot, thinly sliced
1 tsp. dried sage
1 tsp. dried thyme
salt and freshly ground pepper to taste
4–6 cups diced cooked turkey or chicken
1/4 cup chopped fresh dill

Melt butter in a large skillet over medium heat and sauté mushrooms until lightly golden. In a large saucepan, heat soup and sherry over medium-low heat, stirring to blend and remove any lumps.

Add vegetables and seasonings to soup mixture. Reduce heat, stir and simmer for 10 or 15 minutes. Add turkey and dill and cook for 10 minutes.

Freeze in containers or plastic freezer bags.

To reheat on the stovetop or in the microwave, see pages 5 and 6. Use water or sherry. If adding sherry during cooking, be sure to continue simmering for a few minutes.

TURKEY IN ROSEMARY ORANGE SAUCE

Servings: 4

Orange juice adds a nice flavor to poultry. Try this and you'll become slightly addicted, as I am.

4 turkey cutlets, about 2 lb., or 4 boneless, skinless chicken breast halves
salt and freshly ground pepper to taste
3 tbs. vegetable oil, divided
1/4 cup finely chopped shallots
3 cloves garlic, minced
3/4 cup orange juice
1/2 cup chicken broth
1 tsp. butter or margarine
1 tsp. chopped fresh rosemary
1/2 tsp. wine vinegar

Season both sides of turkey with salt and pepper. In a large skillet over medium-high heat, heat ½ of the oil. Add turkey and sear until well browned on both sides. Remove and set aside.

Reduce heat to medium and add remaining oil. When hot, add shallots and garlic. Cook, stirring, for about 1 minute. Add orange juice and broth. Bring to a simmer and cook until reduced by half, about 3 minutes.

Return turkey to pan, along with any juices that have accumulated. Reduce heat to a simmer and cook until turkey is done.

Add butter, rosemary and vinegar to pan and stir well into sauce. Add additional salt and freshly ground pepper to taste if needed.

Freeze in containers.

To reheat on the stovetop or in the microwave, see pages 5 and 6.

TURKEY ABBONDANZA

"Abbondanza" is Italian for "plenty." The green okra, peppers and celery contrast with the rich red sauce to make this attractive as well as tasty.

2 tbs. olive oil
1 chicken, quartered, or 4 favorite
  pieces (leg or breast quarters), or use
  turkey cutlets
2 cups commercially prepared
  marinara sauce
1/2 cup red wine

1 green bell pepper, diced
1 lb. okra, ends removed, sliced
1 cup thinly sliced celery
2 onions, chopped
1/2 tsp. dried basil
1/2 tsp. dried oregano
1/2 lb. mushrooms, sliced

Heat oven to 350°. Heat oil in a large skillet over medium heat. Place turkey in skillet and cook, turning, until browned.

Mix all remaining ingredients except mushrooms in a baking pan large enough to hold turkey pieces in one layer. When turkey is browned, remove from skillet and place pieces in baking pan. Add mushrooms to skillet and sauté until lightly golden. Remove mushrooms and distribute evenly in baking pan. Bake for 40 minutes, or until turkey tests done.

Freeze in plastic freezer bags.

To reheat on the stovetop or in the microwave, see pages 5 and 6.

MICHIGAN POULTRY STEW

This Midwestern dish is hearty, slightly sweet, and bound to please your family, your guests and yourself.

2 tbs. butter
2 medium red onions, coarsely chopped
4 cloves garlic, coarsely chopped
3 carrots, peeled and cut into thick slices
4 large potatoes, peeled and cut into eighths
1 tsp. dried savory
1/4 tsp. dried marjoram

2 lb. boneless, skinless chicken breast halves or turkey cutlets, cut into smaller pieces
2 tsp. red wine vinegar
1 tsp. brown sugar
4 cups chicken broth
1/2 cup dry white wine
2 pinches cayenne pepper
salt to taste

In a Dutch oven or similar pot, melt butter over low heat. Add onions and garlic, cover and cook for 10 minutes. Remove lid and add carrots and potatoes. Stir, cover and cook for 15 minutes.

Add all remaining ingredients and cover. Raise heat to medium-low and cook for another 30 minutes, or until potatoes are done. Stir occasionally while cooking.

Freeze in plastic freezer bags.

To reheat on the stovetop or in the microwave, see pages 5 and 6.

PORK, SAUSAGE AND LAMB

PORK MEATBALLS
IN CRANBERRY-TOMATO SAUCE

Servings: 6–8

This flavorful meatball dish is a delicious alternative to ordinary beef meatballs.

2 jars (16 oz. each) medium or hot
   salsa
2 cans (16 oz. each) jellied cranberry
   sauce
3 lb. ground pork
1/2 cup breadcrumbs
2 medium onions, finely diced

3 cloves garlic, pressed
salt and freshly ground pepper to taste
1/2 tsp. dried sage
1/4 tsp. nutmeg
1/8 cup chopped fresh dill
1 egg, beaten
3 tbs. vegetable oil

Over medium heat, combine salsa and cranberry sauce in a Dutch oven or similar large pot. While sauce heats, mix together pork, breadcrumbs, onions, garlic, salt, pepper, sage, nutmeg, dill and egg and blend well.

Heat oil over medium heat in large skillet. Form meat mixture into meatballs and brown meatballs on all sides, transferring to Dutch oven when browned. Cook over medium-low heat for 30 minutes.

Freeze in containers or in plastic freezer bags.

To reheat on the stovetop or in the microwave, see pages 5 and 6.

MAPLE PORK TENDERLOIN

The sweet flavors of orange juice and maple syrup complement this lean cut of pork.

1 pork tenderloin, 3/4 lb.
1 medium onion, diced
1/4 cup orange juice, divided
1/4 cup maple syrup, divided
2 tbs. dry white wine
2 tbs. soy sauce
freshly ground pepper to taste
2 cloves garlic, minced
1 tbs. olive oil
1/2 cup chicken broth

Trim any fat from pork. Make a marinade by combining onion, 2 tbs. of the orange juice, 2 tbs. of the maple syrup, wine, soy sauce, pepper and garlic. Mix in a bowl or freezer bag, add tenderloin and cover or seal. Marinate in the refrigerator for at least 2 hours.

Heat oven to 400°. In a medium skillet, heat oil over medium heat. Remove pork from marinade and place in skillet, reserving marinade. Cook for 5 minutes, turning to brown evenly. Transfer pork to a small baking pan and bake for 30 minutes.

About 20 minutes into baking process, pour reserved marinade into a saucepan and add remaining orange juice, remaining maple syrup and broth. Over medium-high heat, bring to a boil, reduce heat and simmer for about 5 minutes, or until sauce thickens slightly. Use as gravy for pork.

Slice into $1/8$-inch rounds and freeze each serving ($1/3$ of the slices with $1/3$ of the sauce) in a plastic freezer bag.

To reheat on the stovetop or in the microwave, see pages 5 and 6.

PORK CHOP CASSEROLE

Here's another all-in-one meal, offering rice, green peppers and pork chops in a tomato-based sauce. Serve this with French bread or garlic bread, with a nice salad or even with an additional vegetable.

1 can (15 oz.) tomato sauce
1 cup red wine
1 tsp. Worcestershire sauce
1/4 tsp. dried marjoram
1/2 tsp. dried savory

1/2 tsp. cayenne pepper
6 pork chops, 1/2-inch thick
1 onion, chopped
2 green bell peppers, diced
2 cups uncooked rice

Heat oven to 350°. Use a baking dish or roasting pan large enough to hold 6 chops in one layer. Pour tomato sauce into baking dish; add wine, Worcestershire, herbs and cayenne and mix. Place chops in baking dish. Add onion, green peppers and rice in sauce around chops.

Cover baking dish with foil and bake for 45 minutes.

Freeze each portion in a plastic freezer bag or in a container.

Reheat in a 350° oven in a baking dish or roasting pan covered tightly with aluminum foil for about 35 minutes.

PORK WITH CUBAN BLACK BEANS

Serve this very rich adaptation of Cuban pork and beans with rice.

2 tbs. peanut oil or other oil
1 onion, diced
1 clove garlic, sliced
1 tsp. hot paprika
1 lb. pork, cut into strips
1/2 cup vegetable or chicken broth
1/2 cup smooth peanut butter, prefer no
  additives

2 cans (15 oz. each) ready-to-eat
  Cuban-style black beans, such as
  Goya brand
1 tbs. finely chopped fresh cilantro
2 tbs. lime juice
1 heaping tsp. curry powder

    Heat oil in a large skillet over medium heat. Add onion and garlic and cook until onion is golden. Add paprika and pork and cook until pork begins to brown.

    Add remaining ingredients, stirring well until pork is cooked through and ingredients are well blended.

    Freeze in containers.

    To reheat on the stovetop or in the microwave, see pages 5 and 6.

GRANNY SMITH PORK STEW

Servings: 6–8

The "granny" in question is an apple. Here, Granny Smith apples, bell peppers, pearl onions and sweet potatoes combine in a special pork dish.

3 cups apple juice
1 cup beef broth
1/2 tsp. ground ginger
1/4 tsp. dried basil
1/2 tsp. dried sage
1/4 tsp. mace
1/8 tsp. ground cloves
1/2 tsp. cayenne pepper
1 cup sherry
3 tbs. vegetable oil
3 lb. pork, cut into 2-inch cubes
2 green bell peppers, cut into bite-sized pieces
1 pkg. (16 oz.) frozen pearl onions or small onions
1 can (15 oz.) sweet potatoes
1 Granny Smith apple or other tart variety

Heat apple juice over medium-low heat in a Dutch oven or similar large pot and add beef broth. Add ginger, basil, sage, mace, cloves, cayenne and sherry. Simmer, uncovered.

Heat oil in a large skillet over medium heat. Add pork and cook until lightly browned. When pork is browned, transfer to Dutch oven. When all pork is in Dutch oven, adjust heat so sauce is simmering, cover and cook for 45 minutes. At end of cooking time, add green pepper pieces, onions and sweet potatoes; cook for 10 minutes.

Peel and core apple and cut into quarters. Cut each quarter into 4 pieces. Add apple to stew and cook for 4 minutes.

Freeze in plastic freezer bags.

To reheat on the stovetop or in the microwave, see pages 5 and 6.

MEDITERRANEAN PORK CHOPS

Servings: 4

Your dish will taste even more Mediterranean if your herbs are fresh. If you have fresh herbs on hand, use triple the dried quantity.

4 lean, thick, preferably center-cut pork chops
salt and freshly ground pepper to taste
2 tbs. olive oil
2 medium onions, finely chopped
4 cloves garlic, minced
1 red bell pepper, cut into bite-sized strips
1 yellow bell pepper, cut into bite-sized strips
1 green bell pepper, cut into bite-sized strips

1 cup chicken broth
2 tbs. red wine vinegar
1 can (15 oz.) crushed tomatoes, with juice
1 tsp. ground cumin
1 bay leaf
1 1/2 tsp. dried rosemary
1 tsp. dried thyme
1 tsp. dried basil
1/2 cup sliced, pitted black olives

Season chops with salt and pepper on both sides. Heat oil over medium-high heat in a skillet large enough to hold all 4 chops at once. Brown chops well on each side. Pour off almost all fat, retaining about 1 tbs., and reduce heat to medium-low. Add onions and garlic and cook until wilted. Add peppers. Cook for 1 minute. Add broth, vinegar, tomatoes, cumin, herbs and additional salt if desired. Reduce heat to low, cover and cook for 20 minutes. Remove from heat, remove bay leaf, and add olives.

Freeze in plastic freezer bags or in containers.

Heat in a 350° oven in a baking dish or roasting pan tightly covered with aluminum foil for 25 to 40 minutes.

RED VELVET PORK STEW

For this stew, pork cooks slowly in a luscious tomato sauce.

2 tbs. vegetable oil
2 lb. lean pork, cut into 2-inch cubes
4 cloves garlic, sliced
2 medium onions, sliced
2 stalks celery, sliced
3 tbs. butter
1 lb. mushrooms, sliced
1 can (15 oz.) crushed tomatoes, with juice
2 cans (15 oz. each) tomato sauce
1 green bell pepper, cut into bite-sized strips

1 cup red wine
1 tbs. Worcestershire sauce
1 tbs. chopped fresh cilantro
1/2 tsp. dried turmeric
1 tsp. dried basil
1 tsp. dried oregano
freshly ground pepper to taste
2 small carrots (or 1 large), cut into 1/4-inch slices
1 can (11 oz.) corn kernels

Heat oil in a large skillet over medium-high heat. Brown pork cubes on all sides, transferring to a Dutch oven or similar large pot when browned. Sauté garlic and onions until beginning to brown, transferring to large pot as they finish. Sauté celery for 2 minutes and add to pot.

Heat butter in skillet and sauté mushrooms; add to large pot. Add all remaining ingredients except corn, bring to a boil, reduce heat, cover and simmer for 1½ hours. When pork is tender, add carrots and corn and cook for 10 minutes.

Freeze in plastic freezer bags.

To reheat on the stovetop or in the microwave, see pages 5 and 6.

CARAWAY PORK CHOPS

Wine and caraway seeds add a distinctive flavor to these chops. Use other fresh herbs besides the dill if you have them on hand—remember, use triple the amount of dried.

2 tbs. peanut oil or other oil
1/2 lb. mushrooms, sliced
2 tsp. paprika
2 tsp. garlic powder
1/2 tsp. dried rosemary
1/2 tsp. dried sage
1/2 tsp. dried thyme
4 boneless pork chops, 1/2-inch thick
1 large onion, diced
1 cup dry white wine
2 tsp. caraway seeds
1/4 cup chopped fresh dill

Heat oil in a large skillet over medium-high heat. Add mushrooms, sautéing until lightly golden. Mix together paprika, garlic powder, rosemary, sage and thyme, and rub mixture into both sides of chops.

Remove mushrooms from skillet and set aside. Reduce heat to medium. Add chops and onion to skillet and brown chops on both sides. Add wine and return mushrooms to pan. Reduce heat until wine just simmers and add caraway seeds. Simmer for 30 to 40 minutes, or until chops are tender. Remove from heat, add dill and stir to mix.

Freeze each chop with sauce in a plastic freezer bag or container.

Reheat in a 350° oven in a baking dish or roasting pan tightly covered with aluminum foil for about 35 minutes.

PORK AND SWEET POTATO STEW

Servings: 6

The prep will go much faster if you can get your supermarket to cube the meat for you. But if they won't, it's still a great recipe and worth the effort.

3 tbs. butter or margarine
1/2 lb. mushrooms
2 large onions, chopped
3 cloves garlic, chopped
1 tbs. olive oil
3 lb. lean pork, trimmed of fat and cut into 2-inch cubes
2 cans (14.5 oz. each) diced tomatoes including juice
1 cup chicken broth
1/2 cup dry white wine
2 bay leaves
1 1/2 tsp. dried sage
salt and freshly ground pepper to taste
2 large sweet potatoes, peeled and cut into bite-sized pieces
1 can (11 oz.) corn kernels

Over medium-high heat in a large skillet, melt butter and sauté mushrooms. When not yet fully browned, add onions and cook until translucent. Transfer mushrooms and onions to a Dutch oven. Add garlic to skillet and cook until just beginning to brown. Remove and add to Dutch oven.

Heat oil in skillet. Brown pork on all sides, removing to Dutch oven as cubes brown. Add tomatoes, broth, wine, bay leaves, sage, salt and pepper. Bring to a boil, reduce heat, cover and simmer for 30 minutes. Add sweet potatoes and corn and cook, covered, for 1 hour, or until pork is tender. Remove bay leaves.

Freeze in individual servings in plastic freezer bags.

To reheat on the stovetop or in the microwave, see pages 5 and 6.

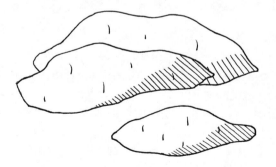

PINEAPPLE PORK CHILI

Here's a new twist on chili — a pork chili, with pineapple and white beans. Pineapple lends a sweet flavor, and you can make the dish as spicy or mild as you wish by using mild or hot chili powder to your taste.

2 tbs. vegetable oil
1 medium onion, chopped
1 lb. lean, boneless pork, trimmed of fat and cut into 1-inch cubes
1 cup dried small white beans, rinsed and drained
2 cups red wine
1 can (14.5 oz.) diced tomatoes, with juice

1 can (6 oz.) tomato paste
1 can (4.5 oz.) chopped green chiles
2–3 tbs. chili powder, mild or hot, to taste
1 tbs. ground cumin
2 tsp. garlic powder
1 can (20 oz.) pineapple chunks, drained, juice reserved

In a small skillet, heat oil over medium heat and sauté onion until golden. Place onion in a large saucepan with all remaining ingredients, except pineapple chunks, but including reserved pineapple juice. Simmer for 3 to 4 hours, or until beans are tender and pork is cooked. Turn off heat and stir in pineapple chunks.

Freeze in containers.

To reheat on the stovetop or in the microwave, see pages 5 and 6.

GOLDEN PORK CHOPS

Peaches complement the pork beautifully in this slightly unusual dish.

2 tbs. vegetable oil
4 medium pork chops, with bones
1 can (8 oz.) tomato sauce
1/4 cup brown sugar, packed
1/2 tsp. cinnamon

1/4 tsp. ground cloves
1/4 cup vinegar
1 can (29 oz.) cling peach halves,
    drained, 1/4 cup syrup reserved
salt and freshly ground pepper to taste

In a large skillet, heat oil over medium heat. Lightly brown pork chops on both sides, pouring off excess fat when browned. While chops are browning, mix tomato sauce, sugar, cinnamon, cloves, vinegar and reserved peach syrup.

Heat oven to 350°. Place browned chops in a baking dish large enough to hold them in a single layer. Pour tomato sauce-syrup mixture over chops and add salt and pepper. Top with peach halves. Cover baking dish with aluminum foil and bake for 25 to 45 minutes (depending on thickness of chops), or until chops are thoroughly cooked.

Freeze chops individually with sauce in plastic freezer bags or in containers.

Reheat in a 350° oven in a baking dish or roasting pan tightly covered with aluminum foil for 25 to 40 minutes, depending on thickness of chops.

FIESTA SAUSAGE

When I cook this, I use turkey kielbasa; you can use pork, beef or turkey as you wish. You may find a pair of tongs is easiest for handling the kielbasa slices.

2 tbs. vegetable oil
1 lb. Italian sausage, cut into 1/2-inch chunks
4 cloves garlic, chopped
2 medium onions, chopped
1/2 cup red wine
1 can (15 oz.) ready-to-eat Cuban-style black beans, such as Goya brand

1 cup canned diced tomatoes, with juice
1/4 cup chopped fresh dill
1 tsp. dried sage
1 large yellow bell pepper, diced
1 cup frozen string beans
salt and freshly ground pepper to taste

Heat oil in a large skillet and brown sausage on both sides. Remove and set aside. Add garlic and onions to pan and cook just until wilted. Drain fat from pan and add wine. Add kielbasa and all remaining ingredients. Lower heat, cover and simmer for 20 minutes.

Freeze in containers or plastic freezer bags.

To reheat on the stovetop or in the microwave, see pages 5 and 6.

SAUSAGE, BEAN AND APPLE CASSEROLE

Servings: 3

This is a sweet and comforting casserole: you'll love it!

1 tbs. vegetable oil
1 lb. pork sausage
1 can (30 oz.) kidney beans, rinsed and drained
1 large baking apple, peeled, cored and sliced
1/3 cup brown sugar
1 large onion, sliced
1/2 cup sliced celery
1/2 cup tomato juice
salt and freshly ground pepper to taste

Heat oven to 350°. In a medium skillet over medium heat, heat oil and cook sausage, crumbling and lightly browning. Drain sausage of fat and transfer to a 9-x-13-inch baking pan. Add remaining ingredients and mix well.

Cover baking pan with aluminum foil and bake for 45 minutes. Remove cover and bake for an additional 15 minutes.

Freeze in plastic freezer bags.

To reheat on the stovetop or in the microwave, see pages 5 and 6. If reheating in the oven, be sure to cover container tightly.

KIELBASA MEAL-IN-A-POT

Everyone will be back for seconds — guaranteed! Choose turkey, beef or pork kielbasa.

2 tbs. butter
1 medium onion, coarsely chopped
2 cups chicken or vegetable broth
1/2 cup water
1 lb. kielbasa, cut into 1/2-inch-thick slices
3 potatoes, thinly sliced

2 apples, peeled, cored and cut into 1/2-inch dice
1 pkg. (8 oz.) coleslaw mix (shredded cabbage and carrots)
1/4 tsp. cinnamon
1/2 tsp. dried thyme
1/2 tsp. dried savory

In a Dutch oven or other large pot, heat butter over medium heat and sauté onion until golden. Add broth and water. Add all other ingredients. Simmer, covered, for 45 minutes.

Freeze in containers.

To reheat on the stovetop or in the microwave, see pages 5 and 6. If reheating in the oven, be sure to cover container tightly.

HOT DOG AND BEAN CASSEROLE

Here's an old favorite dressed up with nutritious vegetables.

2 cans (16 oz. each) baked beans
1/3 cup honey
1/2 cup ketchup
1/4 cup vinegar
1 tbs. Worcestershire sauce
1/2 tsp. dried thyme
1/2 tsp. dried oregano
1/2 tsp. dried basil
2 onions, chopped
3 green bell peppers, diced
4 stalks celery, sliced
8 frankfurters, cut into bite-sized pieces

Put all ingredients, except frankfurters, in a Dutch oven or other large pot and simmer for 20 minutes. Add frankfurters and cook for 10 minutes.

Freeze in containers.

To reheat on the stovetop or in the microwave, see pages 5 and 6.

KIELBASA WITH ARTICHOKES AND GARBANZOS

I use turkey kielbasa when I cook this, but it works well with pork, beef or other cooked varieties of sausage.

2 tbs. vegetable oil
1 lb. smoked sausage, cut into 1/2-inch slices
4 cloves garlic, chopped
1/2 lb. mushrooms, sliced
1/2 cup dry white wine
1 can (14 oz.) artichoke hearts, drained and quartered
1/2 tsp. dried sage
1/2 tsp. dried thyme
1/2 tsp. dried rosemary
1/2 tsp. cayenne pepper
1 tbs. caraway seeds
1 cup canned garbanzo beans
1/2 cup chicken broth
2 tbs. vegetable oil

Heat 2 tbs. oil in a large skillet over medium heat. Add sliced sausage and brown on both sides, transferring to a plate as they brown. Add garlic and cook just until wilted, about 1 or 2 minutes. Set aside sausage and garlic. To same skillet, add mushroom and sauté until lightly browned.

Drain fat from pan and add wine. Reduce heat, bring wine to a simmer, and return sausage and garlic to pan. Add all remaining ingredients. Simmer for 10 minutes.

Freeze in containers or plastic freezer bags.

To reheat on the stovetop or in the microwave, see pages 5 and 6.

MISSISSIPPI RED BEANS AND RICE WITH SAUSAGE

Servings: 6

Did you know if you rinse and drain canned beans before using them, you remove a lot of the gas-causing properties? Rinsed beans also absorb more of the other flavors in your recipe.

2 tbs. olive oil
3 medium onions, peeled and thinly sliced
4 cloves garlic, minced
1 large green bell pepper, cut into small dice
1 lb. kielbasa or other cooked sausage, cut into 1/4- to 1/2-inch pieces
3 cans (15 oz. each) kidney beans, rinsed and drained

2 cups red wine
1 bay leaf
3 tbs. tomato paste
salt and freshly ground pepper to taste
several drops hot pepper sauce, such as Tabasco Sauce, to taste
1 tsp. Worcestershire sauce
4–5 cups cooked white rice

Heat oil in a large skillet over medium heat. Sauté onions, garlic and green pepper until wilted. Add sausage slices and brown.

Add beans, wine, bay leaf, tomato paste, salt, pepper, hot pepper sauce and Worcestershire sauce. Reduce heat, cover and simmer for at least 1 hour, preferably 2 hours. Stir occasionally and add water if needed. Sauce should be reasonably thick.

Remove bay leaf. Add rice and mix in.

Freeze in containers or plastic freezer bags.

To reheat on the stovetop or in the microwave, see pages 5 and 6.

SAUSAGE AND CHICKEN

If you divide this hearty dish into more than 4 servings, cut chicken into smaller pieces and distribute pieces evenly among servings.

1 chicken, quartered, or 4 favorite pieces (breast or leg quarters)
salt and freshly ground pepper to taste
2 tbs. olive oil
1 lb. mild or hot Italian sausage, cut into 1-inch pieces
1/2 lb. mushrooms, sliced
2 medium onions, diced
2 cloves garlic, sliced
1 shallot, finely chopped
1 bay leaf
1/8 tsp. dried marjoram
1/8 cup fresh dill
1 tbs. flour
1/2 cup chicken broth
1 cup dry red wine

Season chicken with salt and pepper. Heat oil in a large skillet over medium heat. Add chicken skin-side down and sausage pieces. Cook until first side of chicken is browned. Turn sausage pieces to brown on all sides. Turn chicken to brown on second side, cooking for another 15 minutes.

Remove chicken and sausage and set aside. To same skillet, add mushrooms and sauté until beginning to brown. Add onions, garlic, shallot and herbs. Cook, stirring, just until onion is wilted.

Sprinkle evenly with flour and blend in. Add broth and wine, blending again and scraping up any brown bits from bottom of pan. Return sausage and chicken, skin-side down, to skillet with any accumulated juices. Reduce heat to medium-low and cover. Cook for 15 minutes, or until chicken tests done. Remove bay leaf.

Freeze in plastic freezer bags.

Reheat in a 350° oven in a baking dish or pan large enough to hold chicken in one layer. Cover tightly with aluminum foil and heat for about 45 minutes.

SAUSAGE RAGOUT

You can make this with a variety of sausages for interest — make sure you use all precooked sausages together, or all fresh together, to cook evenly. Try smoked sausages or other varieties available, such as chicken-apple or duck.

1 tbs. olive oil
½ lb. mushrooms, sliced or chopped
1 lb. sausages, any variety or mixed, cut into ½-inch slices
2 cloves garlic, coarsely chopped
1 medium onion, chopped
1 can (15 oz.) cannellini beans, rinsed and drained
1½ cups chicken broth
1 tsp. dried sage
salt and freshly ground pepper to taste

Heat oil in a large skillet over medium heat. Add mushrooms and cook until lightly browned; remove and set aside. Add sausage, garlic and onion to skillet. Stir and turn meat as mixture cooks, browning sausage slices on both sides.

Add beans, chicken broth, sage, salt and pepper. Bring to a boil, reduce heat and simmer until flavors are well blended and liquid thickens, about 20 minutes. Add mushrooms and cook for 5 minutes.

Freeze in containers.

To reheat on the stovetop or in the microwave, see pages 5 and 6.

PORK SAUSAGE WITH APPLE AND CURRY

Servings: 4

Bulk pork sausage, often served for breakfast, pairs with apple and curry to become a dinner entrée.

cooking spray
2 large baking apples, peeled, cored
   and sliced
1 lb. pork sausage
3/4 tsp. curry powder

1/2 tsp. cinnamon
freshly ground pepper to taste
2 tsp. flour
1/2 cup water

Spray a large, preferably nonstick skillet with cooking spray. Over medium-low heat, cook sliced apples for 1 to 2 minutes, stirring them and breaking them up into smaller pieces as they cook. When they are softened, add sausage. Break it up as it cooks, cooking until well crumbled and all pink is gone. Add curry, cinnamon and pepper, and stir well. Reduce heat to low and cook for 2 more minutes.

Combine flour and water in a small bowl and blend well. Add mixture to skillet and stir, blending flour mixture with meat mixture thoroughly. Continue stirring as it cooks for 2 more minutes; mixture will thicken.

Freeze in plastic freezer bags.

To reheat on the stovetop or in the microwave, see pages 5 and 6.

LAMB ALLEGRA

Some traditional Turkish flavors are found in this dish.

1 can (16 oz.) tomato sauce
1/2 cup red wine
1 tbs. Worcestershire sauce
1 lb. ground lamb
1 onion, chopped
3 cloves garlic, chopped
1 cup cooked rice
salt and freshly ground pepper to taste
1 tsp. dried basil

1 tsp. dried oregano
1 tsp. dried rosemary
1/4 cup chopped fresh dill
1/4 cup freshly grated ginger
1/2 cup sliced, pitted kalamata olives
1 small eggplant, peeled, thinly sliced
and slices quartered
1/2 cup plain yogurt
1 cup crumbled feta cheese

Heat oven to 350°. In a bowl, combine tomato sauce, wine and Worcestershire sauce.

Place lamb, onion, garlic, rice, seasonings and olives in a 9-x-13-inch baking pan. Add ½ of the tomato sauce mixture and knead together thoroughly with your hands.

Press ½ of the meat mixture evenly into pan. Layer eggplant evenly over meat. Press remaining meat mixture over eggplant.

Add yogurt and feta cheese to remaining tomato sauce mixture, stirring to combine. Spread it over meat mixture. Bake for 1 hour. Cut into servings with a pancake turner.

Freeze each portion wrapped in aluminum foil.

Reheat in a 350° oven in same foil on a baking sheet for about 40 minutes.

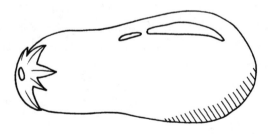

LAMB STEW WITH GREEN BEANS

Serve with boiled potatoes or hot rice and chutney.

3 tbs. olive oil
1 large onion, thinly sliced
4 cloves garlic, minced
3 lb. lamb, trimmed of fat and cubed
2 cans (14.5 oz. each) diced tomatoes, with juice
3 bay leaves
1 tbs. lemon juice

1 tbs. paprika
1 tsp. celery salt
$\frac{1}{2}$ tsp. ground cumin
$\frac{1}{8}$ tsp. cayenne pepper
1 dash ground allspice
1 dash cinnamon
1 $\frac{1}{2}$ lb. green beans, ends trimmed, cut in half if long

Heat oil in a large skillet with a tight-fitting lid over medium heat. Add onion and sauté until golden. Add garlic and lamb, turning cubes to brown on all sides. Add tomatoes, bay leaves, lemon juice and spices. Reduce heat, cover and simmer for about 2 hours. As mixture cooks, check liquid occasionally and add water or wine if needed. About 30 minutes before lamb is done, add beans. Stew is done when lamb is tender. Remove bay leaves.

Freeze in plastic freezer bags.

To reheat on the stovetop or in the microwave, see pages 5 and 6.

TURKISH-STYLE MEATBALLS

For meatballs with a difference, use lamb and rice instead of beef and bread-crumbs. These Turkish-style meatballs don't have a sauce, but they're moist and fla-vorful. They taste good in pita bread with a little minted yogurt and fresh tomatoes.

4 cups water
1 lb. lean ground lamb
1 medium onion, finely chopped
1/4 cup uncooked rice

salt and freshly ground pepper to taste
1 cup olive oil or other oil
2 eggs, beaten

Put 4 cups water in a saucepan over medium heat. Mix together meat, onion, rice, salt and pepper and knead until well mixed. Form into meatballs about 1 inch in diameter. Recipe should make about 16 meatballs.

When water comes to a boil, add meatballs and reduce heat. Simmer, uncovered, for 30 minutes, adding hot water if needed. Remove meatballs and set aside.

Heat oil over medium-high heat in a skillet large enough to hold all meatballs. When surface of oil shimmers, dip meatballs in beaten egg and carefully put them in hot oil. Fry for 5 minutes, turning as needed to brown all sides. Drain.

Freeze each serving wrapped in aluminum foil.

Reheat in a 350° oven in aluminum foil on a baking sheet for about 25 minutes.

LAMB-STUFFED EGGPLANT

Succulent lamb is served in eggplant shells. This different and impressive dish is good enough for company, and you deserve it yourself. Be careful when you score the eggplant flesh not to pierce the skin.

1/2 cup uncooked rice
2 medium or large eggplants
salt to sprinkle on eggplants, plus more for seasoning
1 tbs. olive oil
1 1/2 cups finely chopped onion
2 tsp. finely chopped garlic
1 1/4 lb. ground lamb
3/4 cup cubed fresh tomato
juice of 1 lemon
1/4 cup finely chopped fresh dill
1/4 cup chopped fresh parsley
freshly ground pepper to taste
1/4 cup grated Parmesan cheese, or 8 tbs. crumbled feta cheese

Heat oven to 400°. Cook rice according to package directions.

Halve eggplants lengthwise. Make eggplant shells: With a sharp knife on the cut side of each eggplant half, cut a line about ½ inch to 1 inch in from skin all around the edge. Score the flesh inside this line in a cross-hatch pattern, leaving a ½-inch to 1-inch shell; be careful not to pierce the skin.

Sprinkle exposed eggplant flesh with salt and place halves cut-side up on a rimmed baking sheet or in a baking dish. Bake for 15 minutes.

While eggplant is baking, heat oil in a large skillet over medium heat. Add onion and garlic and cook until wilted. Add lamb and break up as it cooks, until all pink is gone. Add tomato. Stir, cover and cook for about 10 minutes.

Remove eggplants from oven and set temperature to 375°.

With a spoon, carefully remove scored eggplant flesh, being careful to maintain the shell. Coarsely chop removed eggplant flesh and add to lamb mixture. Add lemon juice, dill, parsley, pepper and additional salt if desired. Stir in cooked rice.

Return eggplant halves to baking sheet or baking dish, open-side up, and fill with lamb mixture, mounding in the center. Sprinkle tops with cheese and bake for 30 minutes.

Freeze each portion wrapped in aluminum foil.

To reheat on the stovetop or in the microwave, see pages 5 and 6.

MOROCCAN-STYLE LAMB STEW

Middle-Eastern flavors and unusual ingredients enhance this lamb dish. Serve with hot rice.

1/4 cup olive oil
2 1/2 lb. boneless lamb shoulder, cut into 1 1/2-inch cubes
4 medium onions, quartered
2 tbs. finely chopped fresh ginger
2 cloves garlic, pressed
1/4 cup chopped fresh parsley
salt and freshly ground pepper to taste
1/4 tsp. ground turmeric
1 can (14.5 oz.) diced tomatoes, with juice
1 cup raisins
2 tbs. butter or margarine
2/3 cup almonds
2 hard-cooked eggs

In a Dutch oven or large pot with a tight-fitting lid, heat oil over medium heat. Cook lamb, turning to brown on all sides. Remove lamb from pot and set aside. Add onions, ginger and garlic. Sauté, stirring, until onion is richly golden.

Add parsley, salt, pepper and turmeric and mix well. Return lamb to pot. Stir in tomatoes and juice. Bring to a boil, reduce heat, cover and simmer for 75 minutes, stirring occasionally.

While meat mixture is cooking, plump raisins: put them in a small bowl and cover with warm water. Chop hard-cooked eggs. Toast almonds in a dry skillet over medium heat, tossing and turning to prevent burning, for about 4 minutes or until they become fragrant.

At end of cooking time, test meat for tenderness by piercing with a fork. When meat is done, turn off heat and mix in drained raisins, eggs and almonds.

Freeze in plastic freezer bags.

To reheat on the stovetop or in the microwave, see pages 5 and 6.

GREEK LAMB

This lamb dish is elegant and will bring rave reviews when you serve it to friends and family.

3 lb. boneless lamb, leg or shoulder
1 tbs. olive oil
2 onions, sliced
6 cloves garlic, chopped
1 tbs. tomato paste
2 tsp. grated lemon zest
1 tsp. dried oregano
1 tsp. crumbled dried rosemary
1 pinch allspice
1 pinch cinnamon
2 cups chicken broth
1 can (14 oz.) unmarinated artichoke hearts, drained and quartered
1/2 cup crumbled feta cheese

Heat oven to 500°. Trim lamb of all fat and brown in the oven in a shallow roasting pan for 5 minutes; turn lamb over and brown other side for 5 minutes.

Heat oil over medium heat in a large saucepan. Cook onions just until softened and stir in garlic, tomato paste, lemon zest, herbs and spices. Cook for 1 minute. Add chicken broth and bring to a boil; immediately remove from heat. Add artichokes.

Pour sauce mixture over lamb and cover roasting pan with foil. Set oven to 325° and return lamb to oven. Cook for 3½ hours.

Remove lamb from oven and drain juices from roasting pan. Skim off fat and boil juices for 10 minutes to reduce. Remove from heat and stir in feta cheese.

Slice lamb before freezing. Freeze individual servings in juices in plastic freezer bags or containers.

To reheat on the stovetop or in the microwave, see pages 5 and 6.

HAM IN FRUITED MUSTARD SAUCE

Servings: 4

Many supermarkets sell cubed, cooked ham, which will save a little cutting time. Or, if you have leftovers, this recipe is a great way to use them up. Serve over rice or pasta.

1 cup jellied cranberry sauce
1 cup applesauce
1 cup cider vinegar
1/4 cup Dijon mustard

6 tbs. butter
freshly ground pepper to taste
2 lb. cooked ham, cubed, about 4 cups
1 green bell pepper, diced

Place cranberry sauce, applesauce, vinegar, mustard, butter and pepper in a skillet or saucepan. Over medium-low heat and stirring intermittently, cook until cranberry sauce has dissolved and blends well with the other ingredients. Mixture will thicken. Add ham and bell pepper. Continue cooking just long enough for ham to heat through.

Freeze in plastic freezer bags.

To reheat on the stovetop or in the microwave, see pages 5 and 6.

BEEF AND VEAL

BEEF AURORA

Here's a quick, easy, almost foolproof recipe. The result is a hearty, flavorful, filling dish that's as popular with kids as adults.

salt
1 lb. ground beef
3 tbs. butter or margarine
$1/2$ lb. sliced mushrooms
1 can (10.5 oz.) condensed onion soup, undiluted
generous amount freshly ground pepper to taste
$1/2$ tsp. dried oregano

Salt the bottom of a large, preferably nonstick skillet over medium heat. Add beef, breaking up and stirring until brown. Remove beef from skillet and set aside. Add butter to skillet and heat; add mushrooms and sauté until lightly browned on both sides. Return beef to pan and add onion soup. Add pepper and oregano. Reduce heat and simmer for 10 minutes.

Freeze in containers or plastic freezer bags.

Reheat on the stovetop in a skillet or saucepan over medium heat. Add $1/8$ cup water, cover and stir occasionally for about 15 minutes.

OLD-FASHIONED POT ROAST

Ginger enhances the flavor of this pot roast. You don't need salt — there is enough in the soup. This goes well with noodles or potato pancakes.

2 lb. beef brisket
2 cans (10.5 oz. each) condensed
   onion soup, undiluted
1 cup water
$\frac{1}{2}$ cup red wine
$\frac{1}{3}$ cup tomato paste

$\frac{1}{4}$ cup grated fresh ginger
2 tsp. paprika
6 cloves garlic, halved
freshly ground pepper to taste
2 bay leaves
$\frac{1}{2}$ tsp. dried oregano

Put all ingredients in a Dutch oven or large pot. Cover and simmer for at least 3 hours, until meat is tender. Check occasionally and add water if necessary. Remove bay leaves.

Slice meat before freezing with sauce in containers or freezer bags.

Reheat on the stovetop in a covered pot over medium-low to medium heat for 10 minutes, or longer depending on number of servings.

BEEF GOULASH BRATISLAVA-STYLE

A hearty plate of goulash is a satisfying dinner at any time, and especially in winter. Serve this with noodles, garlic bread or another starch to soak up the rich gravy.

3 tbs. vegetable oil, divided
2 strips bacon, finely diced
2 large onions, chopped
1 green bell pepper, diced
1 medium tomato, chopped
3 cloves garlic, diced
1 1/2 tbs. paprika
1 tsp. caraway seeds
salt and freshly ground pepper to taste
2 1/2 cups water, divided
2 lb. beef, cut into bite-sized cubes
2 tbs. flour

In a large skillet over medium heat, heat 1 tbs. of the oil. Add bacon, stirring, and cook until lightly browned. Add onion, green pepper, tomato, and garlic and sauté for 2 minutes. Transfer to a Dutch oven or other large pot. Add paprika, caraway seeds, salt and pepper. Mix thoroughly. Add $1/2$ cup of water, bring to a boil and reduce to a simmer.

In same skillet, heat remaining 2 tbs. oil over medium heat. Add beef, browning lightly on all sides. As beef cubes brown, transfer them to Dutch oven. Make sure there is at least $1/2$ inch of liquid in pot and that it is simmering; stir and cover.

Cook for about $1 1/2$ hours. Check liquid level occasionally during cooking process and add water if needed. When meat is tender, add flour, stir until smooth and add remaining 2 cups water. Cook for 2 to 3 minutes, until gravy thickens.

Freeze in plastic freezer bags.

To reheat on the stovetop or in the microwave, see pages 5 and 6.

MEDITERRANEAN STEW

This stew requires planning ahead — the meat needs to marinate for at least 24 hours.

1 ½ cups red wine, prefer hearty Burgundy or Merlot
4 cloves garlic, thinly sliced
1 tsp. dried basil
salt to taste
red pepper flakes to taste
2 lb. beef, cut into ½-inch cubes
3 carrots, cut into thin slices
1 large onion, chopped
1 lb. mushrooms, sliced
6 plum tomatoes, or 4 regular tomatoes, coarsely chopped
1 cup pitted kalamata olives
1 tsp. dried oregano
1 tsp. dried basil
1 tsp. dried thyme
½ tsp. dried savory
2 bay leaves
1 cup vegetable or beef broth

In a bowl, mix together wine, garlic, basil, salt and pepper flakes. Add meat, making sure it is well soaked with marinade. Cover bowl and refrigerate for 24 hours or up to 3 days.

Put meat and marinade into the bottom of a Dutch oven or similar large pot. Add all remaining ingredients. Cook over medium heat until mixture starts to boil. Reduce heat, cover and simmer for about 3 hours, or until meat is so tender that you can separate it with a fork. Check liquid level several times during cooking process, and add more broth, water or wine if needed. Remove bay leaves.

Freeze in plastic freezer bags.

To reheat on the stovetop or in the microwave, see pages 5 and 6.

GROUND BEEF GUMBO

Here's a new way to spice up ground beef. Serve this over rice or pasta.

2 tbs. vegetable oil
1 1/2 lb. ground beef
2 medium onions, chopped
2/3 cup sliced celery
2/3 cup diced green bell pepper
3 cloves garlic, minced
1 can (14.5 oz.) diced tomatoes, with juice
1 can (15 oz.) tomato sauce
2 cans (6 oz. each) tomato paste

1/2 lb. mushrooms, sliced
3/4 lb. okra, ends removed, larger pieces halved
2 bay leaves
2 tsp. dried basil
1 tsp. dried tarragon
1 tsp. chili powder
1/2 tsp. ground cumin
salt and freshly ground pepper to taste
1/2 cup red wine

Heat oil in a Dutch oven or large pot over medium heat. Add beef, onion, celery, green pepper and garlic, stirring to break up meat. When meat is browned, drain fat from pot.

Stir in all remaining ingredients and simmer, uncovered, for 1 hour. Remove bay leaves.

Freeze in containers or plastic freezer bags.

To reheat on the stovetop or in the microwave, see pages 5 and 6.

BEEF ROMANA PICANTE

Though this is easy to cook, the result is hearty and flavorful, with just a little bit of "bite." Go ahead, bite back — you'll like it.

salt
1 lb. ground beef
2 cloves garlic, chopped
1 large onion, diced
1/4 cup red wine
1/4 cup chopped, pitted black olives

1/4 cup chopped, pitted green olives
1 can (14.5 oz.) diced tomatoes
1/2 tsp. dried rosemary
1/2 tsp. dried thyme
1 can (4.5 oz.) chopped green chiles

Salt the bottom of a large, preferably nonstick skillet over medium heat. Add beef, breaking up and stirring until browned. Add garlic and onion. Cook, stirring intermittently, until onion and garlic are wilted. Add wine and reduce heat until liquid is just simmering. Add remaining ingredients and simmer for about 7 minutes.

Freeze in containers or plastic freezer bags.

To reheat on the stovetop or in the microwave, see pages 5 and 6.

STUFFED PEPPERS

This is one of the first things I ever learned to cook. It's still easy, hearty and appealing, and it pleases the average man, if you happen to be cooking for one. Improve it with fresh herbs, if you have them — just use triple the amount of dried.

4 firm, flat-bottomed, large green bell peppers
3 cans (8 oz. each) tomato sauce
1 tbs. Worcestershire sauce
1 1/2 tsp. dried basil
1 1/2 tsp. dried oregano
salt and freshly ground pepper to taste
4 cloves garlic, pressed
1 lb. ground beef
3/4 cup cooked rice
1 medium onion, chopped

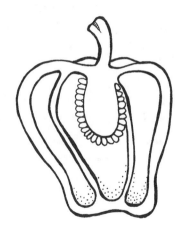

Heat oven to 350°. Slice tops from green peppers and scoop out seeds and ribs. Place upright in a large pot with enough water to cover and simmer until crisp-tender, about 8 minutes. Do not overcook. Place upright in a baking pan or a casserole just large enough to hold them.

In a bowl, mix together tomato sauce, Worcestershire sauce, basil, oregano, salt and pepper to taste and $1/4$ of the pressed garlic. Mix well.

In another bowl, mix together meat and rice. Add $3/4$ cup of the tomato sauce mixture, remaining garlic and onion. Knead together until well mixed. Fill peppers with meat-rice mixture, mounding if necessary. Pour remaining tomato sauce mixture over and around stuffed peppers.

Bake, uncovered, for 50 to 55 minutes.

Freeze in individual containers tall enough to hold peppers.

To reheat on the stovetop or in the microwave, see pages 5 and 6.

EASY BEEF GOULASH

This recipe is made easy with prepared gravies. It also easily becomes beef Stroganoff: used sliced beef, reduce amount of tomato sauce, add some dill, and add a pint of sour cream after removing from heat. If you freeze beef Stroganoff, add the sour cream after reheating process — do not add before freezing. Serve with hot noodles or garlic bread.

3 tbs. vegetable oil
4 medium onions, chopped
3 green bell peppers, cut into bite-sized strips
2 lb. mushrooms, sliced
2 lb. beef round steak, cubed
salt and freshly ground pepper to taste
2 cans (about 10.25 oz. each) beef gravy

2 cans (about 10.25 oz. each) mushroom gravy
1 can (15 oz.) tomato sauce
garlic powder to taste
2 tsp. dried oregano
5 drops hot pepper sauce, such as Tabasco Sauce
2 tbs. Worcestershire sauce
1/2 cup red wine

Heat oil in a large skillet over medium heat. Sauté onions until lightly golden and transfer to a Dutch oven or large pot. Put green pepper strips in skillet, cook just until wilted, and transfer to Dutch oven. Sauté mushrooms until they begin to turn brown and transfer to Dutch oven. Brown meat, seasoning with salt and pepper to taste. Transfer to Dutch oven.

Add all remaining ingredients and simmer, covered, for about 1 1/2 hours, until meat is tender and flavors have blended. Check gravy consistency periodically and add water if needed. If too thin, remove lid at end of cooking period to reduce.

Freeze in plastic freezer bags.

To reheat on the stovetop or in the microwave, see pages 5 and 6.

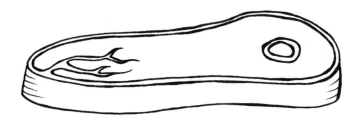

MEATBALLS SWEDISH-STYLE

Servings: 6

Applesauce is an unusual ingredient in these meatballs. You can substitute ground pork or turkey for part of the beef in this recipe.

MEATBALLS

2 lb. ground beef
1 cup cooked rice
2 cups applesauce

2 medium onions, grated
1 1/2 tsp. salt
freshly ground pepper to taste

SAUCE

1 beef bouillon cube
1 tbs. hot water
1 cup tomato sauce
1/2 cup red wine
1 tsp. ground coriander

1 tsp. garlic powder
1/2 tsp. dried thyme
1/2 tsp. dried oregano
1 tsp. brown sugar

Heat oven to 350°. Knead together all meatball ingredients. Form into medium-sized meatballs and place in a roasting pan or baking pan large enough to hold in one layer, preferably not touching.

Dissolve bouillon cube in water, crushing with a spoon and stirring. Mix with remaining sauce ingredients. Pour sauce over meatballs. Bake for 1 hour.

Freeze in plastic freezer bags.

To reheat on the stovetop or in the microwave, see pages 5 and 6.

PARTY BEEF IN WINE SAUCE

Servings: 8

I first tasted this at a party years ago, and the hostess gave me the recipe. Your friends and family will enjoy it, as mine do. Serve over hot noodles or herbed rice.

flour, salt, and freshly ground pepper for dredging
1/4 cup olive oil
2 tbs. butter or margarine
2 large or 3 medium onions, minced
4 cloves garlic, pressed
3 lb. top round steak, cubed

1 beef bouillon cube dissolved in 1 cup water
2 cups dry red wine, prefer Merlot or Cabernet Sauvignon
1/4 tsp. dried oregano
1 bay leaf

Mix salt and pepper to taste in enough flour to coat meat. Heat olive oil and butter over medium heat in a large skillet. Sauté onions and garlic until transparent and transfer to a Dutch oven or large pot. Dredge meat, brown quickly in skillet and transfer to Dutch oven.

Add remaining ingredients to Dutch oven, cover tightly and simmer for about 2 hours, or until meat is tender. Check periodically and add water if sauce becomes too thick. Remove bay leaf.

Freeze in containers or in plastic freezer bags.

To reheat on the stovetop or in the microwave, see pages 5 and 6.

CHEESY BEEF BASTILLE

If you like cheeseburgers, you are guaranteed to like this dish. The paprika is spicy without being too hot, but you can adjust the amount to suit yourself.

2 tbs. vegetable oil
2 medium onions, chopped
1 lb. ground beef
2 tsp. hot paprika
salt to taste
1/4 cup chopped fresh dill

1 tsp. dried savory
1/2 cup red wine
2 tsp. caraway seeds
1 cup grated colby or colby Jack
  cheese

Heat oil in a large skillet over medium heat. Sauté onions until transparent. Add beef, breaking up and stirring; cook until browned. Add paprika, salt, herbs and wine; reduce heat and simmer for 10 minutes. Add caraway seeds and cheese, and cook just until cheese is melted, stirring as it cooks to mix.

Freeze in containers or plastic freezer bags.

Reheat on the stovetop for 10 to 15 minutes; see pages 5 and 6.

DILLY BEEF WITH BLACK BEANS

The odd-sounding mixture of beef, black beans, blue cheese and dill works well in this recipe.

salt
1 lb. ground beef
1 large onion, diced
1 can (15 oz.) black beans, rinsed and drained

1/2 cup crumbled blue cheese
1/4 tsp. cayenne pepper
1/4 tsp. dried oregano
1/8 cup chopped fresh dill

Salt the bottom of a large, preferably nonstick skillet and heat over medium heat. Add beef, breaking up and stirring until browned. Add onion and cook, stirring intermittently, until onion is wilted but not browned.

Reduce heat to medium-low. Add black beans, blue cheese, cayenne, oregano and dill, stirring frequently until cheese is melted and blended in.

Freeze in containers or plastic freezer bags.

To reheat on the stovetop or in the microwave, see pages 5 and 6.

GINGER BEEF STRIPS WITH MUSHROOMS

Servings: 6

Here are more East and West flavors in a skillet stir-fry.

3 containers (1 oz. each) dried
  imported mushrooms
2 lb. beef strips, cut into strips
2 tbs. peanut oil
8 cloves garlic, sliced

1/4 cup grated fresh ginger
1/2 cup red wine
5 tbs. soy sauce
1 can (14 oz.) Chinese baby corn,
  drained

Reconstitute mushrooms for 1 hour in a bowl of warm water to cover. While mushrooms are soaking, heat oil in a large nonstick skillet over medium-high heat. Cook beef strips, stirring constantly, until no longer pink. Add garlic and ginger and cook until garlic is wilted. Add wine and soy sauce.

Squeeze mushrooms to remove excess liquid and reserve 1 cup. Add Chinese corn, mushrooms and reserved liquid. Reduce heat and simmer for 5 minutes.

Freeze in containers.

To reheat on the stovetop or in the microwave, see pages 5 and 6.

ZINGY BEEF STEW

This stew is not for the faint of heart — or mouth. It packs a punch. Credit the hot paprika for the wake-up call to your tongue. You can always adjust the heat to your taste.

1/4 cup peanut or canola oil
4 cloves garlic, chopped
4 onions, chopped
3 lb. top round steak, cut into 2-inch cubes
1 lb. mushrooms, sliced
3–4 tsp. paprika, to taste
1 tbs. caraway seeds
2 cups vegetable broth or water
1 can (14.5 oz.) diced tomatoes, with juice

1/3 cup tomato paste
1 cup red wine
2 tsp. brown sugar
1 tbs. dried sage
1 tbs. dried oregano
1 tbs. dried thyme
1 beef bouillon cube
4 green bell peppers, seeds removed, cut into bite-sized pieces
8 red-skinned potatoes

Heat oil over medium heat in a Dutch oven or large pot. Add beef and brown, turning often. When beef is lightly browned, add garlic and onions and cook until wilted. Add mushrooms and cook until lightly browned. Add paprika and caraway seeds and cook for 5 minutes.

Add vegetable broth, tomatoes, tomato paste, wine, sugar, herbs, salt and bouillon cube. Reduce heat, cover and simmer for about 1 hour. Check periodically and add water if needed.

Add peppers and potatoes and cook for 1 additional hour, or until beef is tender and potatoes are cooked.

Freeze in containers or plastic freezer bags.

To reheat on the stovetop or in the microwave, see pages 5 and 6.

PICADILLO À LA CATALANA

This ground beef recipe is rich with Spanish flavors. Serve it with rice.

2 tbs. olive oil
1 small onion, finely chopped
1 lb. ground beef
salt, freshly ground pepper and garlic powder to taste
1/2 bottle (3.5 oz. bottle) capers with all liquid from bottle
1/2 cup raisins
1/2 cup canned diced tomatoes, drained, with 1/3 cup of the canned juice
1/4 cup diced stuffed olives

In a large skillet, heat oil over medium heat and cook onion until soft but not brown. Add meat, breaking up and browning. Add all remaining ingredients, except olives, and cook for 10 minutes. Add olives.
Freeze in containers.
Reheat on the stovetop for about 15 minutes; see pages 5 and 6.

142   BEEF AND VEAL

BLACK BEAN CHILI CON CARNE

Servings: 3

There is no one "right" way to cook chili. It's fun to vary the meat, the beans and the other flavors.

2 tbs. vegetable oil
4 medium onions, coarsely chopped
1 lb. ground beef
1 can (14.5 oz.) diced tomatoes, with juice
1 can (15 oz.) black beans, almost drained

2 heaping tbs. chili powder, or to taste
1/2 tsp. dried oregano
1/2 tsp. garlic powder
salt and freshly ground pepper to taste
cayenne pepper to taste, optional

In a large skillet, heat oil over medium heat and sauté onions until golden. Add beef, breaking it up, and cook until beginning to brown. Add tomatoes with juice and beans with a small amount of juice.

Add remaining ingredients, reduce heat, cover and simmer for about 1 hour. Check periodically and add water if needed. Taste and adjust seasonings if needed. If chili is too soupy, remove lid and cook until liquid level is reduced.

Freeze in containers.

To reheat on the stovetop or in the microwave, see pages 5 and 6.

KOFTA

This Middle-Eastern recipe includes green pepper, tomato and potatoes, as well as the meat—an all-in-one dinner that needs nothing further cooked with it. And it's easy!

1 lb. ground beef
1 onion, finely diced
a few sprigs fresh parsley, finely chopped
salt and freshly ground pepper to taste
2 tbs. olive oil

1 onion, cut into rings
2 potatoes, thinly sliced into circles
1 large green bell pepper, cut into thin rings
1 large tomato, cut into thick round slices

Heat oven to 450°. In a bowl, mix beef, diced onion, parsley, salt and pepper. Oil an 8-x-8-inch or 9-x-9-inch baking pan and place beef mixture in pan, keeping mixture level.

Spread remaining ingredients evenly over beef mixture. Cover pan with aluminum foil and bake for 1 hour.

To freeze, wrap tightly in aluminum foil.

Reheat in same foil in a 350° oven for about 20 to 25 minutes.

VEAL STEW

This recipe, a favorite from my mother, goes nicely with noodles, rice or barley.

3 tbs. vegetable oil
4 medium onions, sliced
4 cloves garlic, chopped
4 lb. veal, cut into 2-inch cubes
salt and freshly ground pepper to taste
1 1/2 cups flour
2 tbs. paprika
1 1/2 tsp. dried basil

1 1/2 tsp. dried thyme
2 tsp. dried rosemary
2 cups chicken broth
1/2 lb. mushrooms, sliced
3 stalks celery, sliced
2 tbs. butter or margarine
2 cups frozen string beans
1 can (15 oz.) crushed tomatoes, with juice

Heat oil in a large skillet over medium heat and cook onion and garlic until wilted. Add veal and cook until no longer pink, stirring often. Blend in salt, pepper and flour, stirring until smooth. Add paprika, herbs and broth. Blend well, cover and simmer for 2 hours, until veal is tender.

Sauté mushrooms and celery separately in butter until mushrooms are lightly browned and celery begins to brown. Add mushrooms, string beans and celery to stew with tomatoes after 2 hours. Cook for 15 minutes.

Freeze in plastic freezer bags.

To reheat on the stovetop or in the microwave, see pages 5 and 6.

FRENCH VEAL CHOPS

Splurge — prepare veal loin chops for a special dinner.

6 tbs. butter or margarine, divided
12 large mushroom caps
3 tbs. olive oil
flour to dredge chops
salt and freshly ground pepper to taste
6 thick veal loin chops
2 medium onions, finely chopped
2 cloves garlic, finely chopped
2 ripe tomatoes, peeled and chopped
$1/2$ cup dry white wine
$1 1/2$ tsp. dried rosemary, crushed
$3/4$ cup small whole pitted Nicoise olives

In a large skillet over medium heat, heat 3 tbs. of the butter. Sauté mushroom caps and set aside. Mix flour, salt and pepper together and dredge chops. Raise heat to medium-high and heat remaining butter and oil. Quickly brown chops on both sides and set aside. Add onions and garlic to skillet and cook until lightly browned. Add tomatoes to skillet and cook for 5 minutes.

Reduce heat. Return chops to skillet and add wine and rosemary. Cover and simmer until chops are tender but not mushy, about 30 minutes. Remove from heat and add olives and mushrooms.

Freeze in plastic freezer bags or in containers.

Reheat in a 350° oven in a baking dish or pan covered tightly with aluminum foil for about 30 minutes.

VEAL MARSALA

This recipe can also be made with chicken or turkey cutlets. Either way, it is elegant enough to serve to guests.

salt and freshly ground pepper to taste
flour to dredge veal
1 1/2 lb. veal cutlets or scallops, pounded
3 tbs. olive oil
1/2 lb. mushrooms
3–5 cloves garlic
2 cups chicken broth
1 cup Marsala wine or dry white wine
1 1/2 tbs. lemon juice
1 pinch dried marjoram
1/2 tsp. dried thyme

Mix salt and pepper with enough flour to coat veal. Dredge veal in flour mixture. Heat oil in a large skillet over medium heat and sauté mushrooms until golden. While sautéing mushrooms, add garlic to wilt but not brown.

When mushrooms and garlic are ready, push them to the side and quickly brown veal on both sides.

When veal is browned, add broth, wine, lemon juice and herbs to the pan. Blend and push garlic and mushrooms back into middle of pan. Reduce heat, cover and simmer for about 30 minutes.

Freeze in containers.

To reheat on the stovetop or in the microwave, see pages 5 and 6.

INDEX

Serve Creative, Easy, Nutritious Meals with nitty gritty® Cookbooks

100 Dynamite Desserts
The 9 x 13 Pan Cookbook
The Barbecue Cookbook
Beer and Good Food
The Best Bagels are Made at Home
The Best Pizza is Made at Home
The Big Book of Bread Machine
    Recipes
Blender Drinks
Bread Baking
Bread Machine Cookbook
Bread Machine Cookbook II
Bread Machine Cookbook III
Bread Machine Cookbook IV
Bread Machine Cookbook V
Bread Machine Cookbook VI
Cappuccino/Espresso
Casseroles
The Coffee Book
Convection Oven Cookery
The Cook-Ahead Cookbook
Cooking for 1 or 2
Cooking in Clay
Cooking in Porcelain

Cooking on the Indoor Grill
Cooking with Chile Peppers
Cooking with Grains
Cooking with Your Kids
The Dehydrator Cookbook
Edible Pockets for Every Meal
Extra-Special Crockery Pot Recipes
Fabulous Fiber Cookery
Fondue and Hot Dips
Fresh Vegetables
From Freezer, 'Fridge and Pantry
From Your Ice Cream Maker
The Garlic Cookbook
Gourmet Gifts
Healthy Cooking on the Run
Healthy Snacks for Kids
The Juicer Book
The Juicer Book II
Lowfat American Favorites
New International Fondue Cookbook
No Salt, No Sugar, No Fat
One-Dish Meals
The Pasta Machine Cookbook

Pinch of Time: Meals in Less than 30
    Minutes
Quick and Easy Pasta Recipes
Recipes for the Loaf Pan
Recipes for the Pressure Cooker
Recipes for Yogurt Cheese
Risottos, Paellas, and other Rice
    Specialties
Rotisserie Oven Cooking
The Sandwich Maker Cookbook
The Sensational Skillet: Sautés and
    Stir-Fries
Slow Cooking in Crock-Pot,® Slow
    Cooker, Oven and Multi-Cooker
Soups and Stews
The Toaster Oven Cookbook
Unbeatable Chicken Recipes
The Vegetarian Slow Cooker
New Waffles and Pizzelles
The Well Dressed Potato
Wraps and Roll-Ups

For a free catalog, call: Bristol Publishing Enterprises, Inc.
(800) 346-4889
www.bristolcookbooks.com